SIMPLE TRADITIONS

SIMPLE TRADITIONS
14 Quilts to Warm Your Home

Kim Diehl

Martingale®
& COMPANY

Simple Traditions: 14 Quilts to Warm Your Home
© 2006 by Kim Diehl

That Patchwork Place® is an imprint of Martingale & Company®.

Martingale & Company
20205 144th Avenue NE
Woodinville, WA 98072-8478 USA
www.martingale-pub.com

Credits

President: Nancy J. Martin
CEO: Daniel J. Martin
COO: Tom Wierzbicki
Publisher: Jane Hamada
Editorial Director: Mary V. Green
Managing Editor: Tina Cook
Technical Editor: Ellen Pahl
Copy Editor: Ellen Balstad
Design Director: Stan Green
Illustrator: Laurel Strand
Cover and Text Designer: Stan Green
Photographer: Brent Kane

Printed in China
11 10 09 08   8 7 6 5 4

Library of Congress Cataloging-in-Publication Data
Library of Congress Control Number: 2006004002

ISBN-13: 978-1-56477-638-9
ISBN-10: 1-56477-638-7

DEDICATION

To the memory of my grandma, who, in her quiet, unassuming way, could do almost anything and do it well.

MISSION STATEMENT
Dedicated to providing quality products and service to inspire creativity.

Acknowledgments

To my quilting friends Terry Anderson, Donna Clayson, Deslynn Mecham, Pat Peyton, Evelyne Schow, Penny Stephenson, and Barb Stommel, words just aren't enough to express my appreciation for all your help in cutting, sewing, trimming, pressing, binding—too many things to list!

For my machine quilters extraordinaire, Celeste Freiberg and Kathy Ockerman, a big thank-you for finishing my quilts so beautifully and with such artistic flair.

To my family, thank you for always being so good-natured and understanding when I spend hours doodling, cutting, and sewing—all the while leaving a trail of fabric scraps, pins, and thread in my wake. Molly Dolly, for a kiddo your color sense is amazing and your skill at removing paper pattern pieces is unparalleled. And Katie Pie, it's been so fabulous having a teenager to drive and deliver my quilts—and you hardly ever get lost!

My sincere and heartfelt thanks to the staff at Martingale & Company for continually providing a professional and encouraging atmosphere that enables me to freely express myself and see my ideas come alive. And all my gratitude to Stan Green and Brent Kane for their exceptional design and photography abilities, which were evident as we photographed the "Plain and Simple" project in Kathy Ockerman's home and all the other projects in my home.

Many thanks to Janome America for the use of your Memory Craft 10001 sewing machine as I constructed the models for this book. Sewing has never been such fun!

Last but not least, I'd like to express my thanks to Fairfield Processing Corporation for your Soft Touch batting, which gives my quilts the softly puckered, antique look that is so reminiscent of my grandma's quilts.

CONTENTS

INTRODUCTION

For as long as I can remember, quilts have been a part of my life. As a young girl, my grandma's softly worn, hand-pieced quilts were always on my bed. I can still recall how it felt to run my fingers over their smooth yet bumpy surfaces as I studied the array of intricate shapes and hundreds of tiny stitches that each one contained. Although they fascinated me, it never occurred to me to wonder how my "blankets" came to be, for they had always just been there, quietly giving me warmth and comfort. Now that I'm older (and maybe a bit wiser), I fully understand the measure of patience and perseverance that making a quilt requires. Each one truly represents a labor of love.

Today I count myself fortunate to be able to carry on the tradition of quiltmaking, and I greatly value the connection it gives me to my grandma.

While growing up on a farm in Texas many years ago, my grandma's supplies were often scarce, so she used every available resource. Quilt patches were often cut from flour sacks and colorful scraps of clothing, and then hand-stitched into traditional patterns that had been handed down by her mother or shared among friends. Many of my grandma's quilts were born of necessity and were meant for everyday use, not fancy decoration, yet that only added to their charm. My grandma once shared with me that she made her quilts as fast as she could because her family needed the blankets, and this self-sufficient upbringing helped to shape her industrious spirit. Throughout her life she never sat idly, and she always had handwork of some sort in her lap.

Many years have passed since my grandma plied her needle and thread, and although she is no longer with me, the love of quilts that she unknowingly instilled in me lives on. I've come to realize that my fondness for scrappy designs and "make do" color schemes is in large part due to her influence and my admiration for women like her who relied on their ingenuity and creative use of fabric when fashioning their beautiful designs.

Today I count myself fortunate to be able to carry on the tradition of quiltmaking, and I greatly value the connection it gives me to my grandma. Innovations she never dreamed of now make it possible for us as modern quilters to assemble our quilts in much less time, but with no less pride and care.

The designs presented in this book are rooted in tradition and were inspired by classic blocks and motifs that have long been favored by quilters. Notice how the fabric and color choices, rather than the traditional designs, seem to ultimately set the tone for each quilt. Notice also that traditional doesn't have to mean stuffy or old-fashioned! Many of these projects will enable you to experiment with color and explore the endless possibilities that your scrap basket can yield, so enjoy yourself and let your creativity flow. The sky's the limit! Your quilts will leave a lasting impression and be enjoyed by generations to come.

Fabric Selection and Preparation

The following sections provide some basic tips for selecting quiltmaking fabrics and choosing project color schemes. The advantages and disadvantages of prewashing your fabrics before you begin a project are also discussed so that you can be informed when deciding your own preferences.

Fabrics for Quiltmaking

Each project in this book was made from 100%-cotton fabrics of high quality. I prefer to use cotton because it retains a crease when pressed, is easily manipulated for appliqué purposes, and is soft and lightweight for quilting.

Prewashing Pros and Cons

Prewashing your fabric will remove the sizing and leave the cloth soft and easy to handle. Washing will also shrink the fabric slightly and remove any excess dye. On the other hand, many quilters prefer not to prewash fabrics because they enjoy the firmer texture that the sizing lends. Another advantage to using fabrics that have not been prewashed is that you can achieve a softly puckered, vintage look if you layer your finished top with unwashed cotton batting and backing, and immerse it in water after quilting.

If you prefer to prewash your fabrics, place them in your washing machine on a warm setting with mild detergent. Dry your fabrics in a dryer on a medium setting until barely damp, and then press them with a hot iron to remove any wrinkles.

If you decide not to prewash, it's a good practice to test dark-hued fabrics that pose a risk of bleeding (such as deep reds) to determine if they are colorfast.

One method of testing is to place a fabric swatch in a bowl of very hot water with a drop of detergent. After several minutes, remove the swatch and place it on two or three layers of white paper towel or muslin to dry. While the fabric is still wet, blot it with the paper towel to see if there is any transfer of color. After the swatch is dry, check the paper towel for any color residue. If you discover a loss of dye during any step of this process, or find color in the bowl of water, I recommend that you choose a different fabric.

Selecting Color Schemes and Prints

Selecting a color scheme and deciding upon specific prints for any project can be a daunting task. In this section I'll share how I developed my sense of color and the guidelines that I use when selecting fabrics. The project directions in this book will provide color choices to duplicate the look of each featured quilt, but I encourage you to give these guidelines a try and have fun personalizing your choices.

When I first discovered quiltmaking, I knew nothing pertaining to color theory and even less about using a color wheel. To remedy this, I set out to educate myself by taking time to look at quilts in books, magazines, and quilt shows.

What a wonderful way to learn! The quilts of others can provide you with endless opportunities to study the way in which various hues and prints work together, and how the scale and color value of each print can change when it's paired with something new. Over time you'll see (as I did) the patterns in your own personal preferences begin to emerge. As you become more attuned to your likes and dislikes, it will become easier to make your fabric selections. And remember, it's only necessary to please yourself!

The following guidelines summarize the approaches that I use when selecting fabrics for my quilts:

- For a more traditional or formal look, choose fewer colors and repeat them throughout the quilt top. One print will usually be used for each color.

- For just a bit of the "make do" look, first select the prints that will make up your main color scheme, and then add several look-alikes. In other words, choose fabrics with similar hues and scale of print to imply that you ran short of your main selections and had to substitute others. This method will make you successful if you're having a difficult time choosing just one perfect print.

- To achieve a planned scrappy look, select your colors and prints as you would for a "make do" quilt. Then add several lighter, brighter, and darker shades, along with a few complementary colors. Vary the size and scale of your prints for added interest. Your choices should appear deliberate.

- For a completely scrappy look, take the above guidelines one step further by throwing in colors and prints that are slightly off, but not glaringly so. Don't feel compelled to use any print or color that you really don't like—life's too short! You can give a sense of balance to these quilts by squinting your eyes and viewing the center to determine a predominant color. Feature that color in your border for a balanced, pulled-together look, or use it alone to calm a boisterous center. If your pattern is becoming lost in a sea of scraps, consider limiting your background prints or try using just one.

- One general rule I've found to be consistently true when choosing colors and prints for my projects, particularly scrap quilts, is that most hues can be intermingled successfully as long as muted, muddy tones are never mixed with clear, bright colors. Keep this simple guideline in mind as you audition your fabrics and you'll find that it really works!

The methods for fabric selection that I've shared above can be incorporated into nearly any quilt and will provide you with endless possibilities. Ultimately, I've learned to trust my instincts when selecting my fabrics, and they've never failed me. So listen to that little voice inside and you'll find that when your choices are right, you'll know it instantly. If you're not sure your choices are right, you need to make changes!

Pin Point

CREATIVE COLOR COMBINATIONS

Try pairing colors and prints that may not seem like obvious combinations when you begin choosing fabrics for a new project, even when a pattern may suggest different hues. You'll often be pleasantly surprised at the outcome, and your quilt will reflect your own unique flair.

Patchwork Principles

Among the topics included in this section are the specific techniques and procedures used to piece and assemble the featured projects. You'll notice that some steps are universally practiced, while others are unique and the result of trial and error as I was teaching myself to make quilts.

 *Pin Point*

New Life for Old Mats

Don't throw out your worn cutting mat! Turn it over and use the reverse side for a nonslip surface when tracing appliqué patterns or drawing stitching lines on patchwork pieces.

Yardage and Piecing Requirements

The project directions in this book are based on 42"-wide fabric and assume a 40" usable width after prewashing. To make the best use of your yardages, always cut the pieces in the order given. All patchwork should be sewn with right sides together unless the directions specify differently.

Rotary Cutting

Unless otherwise instructed, cut all pieces on the straight of grain and across the width of the fabric. To speed the process when cutting a large number of pieces, I fold my fabric in half with the selvages together, and then in half once more. This results in four pieces with each cut. Of course, the size of your pieces will determine how many folds can be made. Fabric that is creased or badly wrinkled should be pressed to lie flat before you begin cutting.

Place your folded fabric on a cutting mat with the fold aligned along a horizontal line of the marked grid. Position your ruler on top of the fabric and place your hand firmly on the ruler, with your pinkie on the cutting mat and against the outside edge of the ruler to prevent the ruler from shifting. Make a vertical cut along one side of your fabric to establish a straight edge. Begin cutting your pieces, measuring from this straight edge.

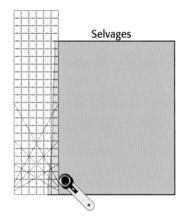

Selvages

To cut half-square triangles from squares, place the square (or layered stack of squares) on your cutting mat. Lay your ruler diagonally over the square with the cutting edge aligned directly over the corners and make the cut.

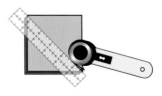

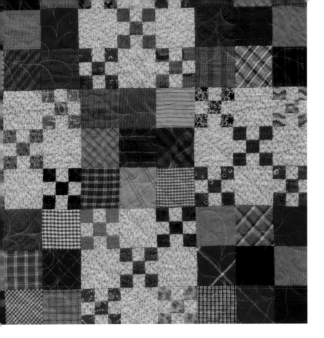

PINNING

As a personal preference, I pin my layered patchwork pieces together before feeding them through the sewing machine. It's a good practice to place pins at even intervals, especially at each sewn seam and intersection. I don't pin pieces at the front edge where they feed under the presser foot because the presser foot will hold them in place. However, I always pin the tail end of my layered patchwork because the back edge will often fishtail, which can cause an inaccurate seam allowance. If you pin this edge using a glass-head pin, you can lay your finger over the pinhead and use it to steer the patchwork through the machine in a straight line.

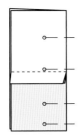

As I stitch toward a pin, I generally don't remove it but instead greatly reduce my speed just as the needle passes over it. Slowing my speed allows the needle to slide over the pin, as opposed to high-speed sewing, which often results in the needle striking the pin and breaking. I prefer this method of pinning and stitching to reduce shifting of the fabric layers in order to achieve accurate seams and sharp points, but ultimately you need to experiment to determine what works well for you and accommodates your sewing machine.

MACHINE PIECING

Always remember to join your fabrics with right sides together unless the directions instruct otherwise. For most projects, your machine's standard stitch length will be fine. However, for smaller-scale patchwork pieces, I recommend reducing your stitch length slightly to achieve more stitches to the inch. Your seams will be secure right to the edge of the joined pieces, and they'll remain invisible even after they've been pressed open.

As you begin sewing a machine-stitched seam, grasp the spool and bobbin threads and pull them gently as the fabric begins to feed under the presser foot. This will enable the fabric to begin feeding smoothly while preventing thread snarls. Never estimate the width of your seam allowance as you stitch, because accurate machine piecing requires that you stitch consistent ¼" seams. If your seam allowance is off by as little as ¹⁄₁₆", this difference will multiply with each sewn seam and can result in finished blocks or entire pieced units that don't fit together. Here are two methods to help you achieve accuracy:

- Use a ¼" presser foot made specifically for quiltmaking.

- Make a visual guide by gently lowering the needle of your sewing machine until the point rests upon the ¼" line of an acrylic ruler. Ensure that the ruler is aligned in a straight position and apply

PERFECTLY ALIGNED PATCHWORK

For patchwork that includes layered triangles or squares that are pinned together and joined with a diagonal seam, try this little trick. Pin the pieces together as usual, and then place a small dot of basting glue within the seam-allowance layers near each point to prevent them from shifting as you stitch. Your stitched patchwork will always have perfectly aligned edges.

PERFECT SEAMS

To increase your accuracy, when you seat yourself at your sewing machine, position your chair squarely in front of the needle. This may seem overly simple, but sitting at even a slight angle to the needle can distort your view as you sew and cause variances in your seam allowances.

a line of ¼" masking tape to the sewing-machine surface exactly along the ruler's edge, taking care not to cover the feed dogs. Align the edge of your fabrics with this taped line when feeding them through the machine.

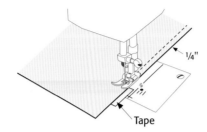

It is a good idea to check the accuracy of your seam allowance from time to time, particularly when beginning a project with small-scale patchwork. This can be done as follows:

1. Cut three rectangles of fabric measuring 1½" x 3", and sew them together side by side along the long edges; press the seam allowances in one direction.

2. The width of the center rectangle should measure 1". If it does not, determine where the discrepancies are occurring and make adjustments.

Another indispensable tip that I use for checking the accuracy of my piecing is to check my seamed patchwork against each measured piece of cloth of the same size as I'm pinning them to be joined. If I note a size difference, I measure the patchwork unit to determine where the discrepancy lies and make corrections before continuing my block assembly.

Before piecing a quilt with complex blocks, I recommend that you make a test block. After the block is complete, measure its size for accuracy and make any necessary adjustments before proceeding. This will save lots of time and frustration when it's time to assemble your blocks into a quilt top.

STRIP PIECING

To simplify the piecing process for patchwork with repeated patterns, such as checkerboards, lengths of fabric can be sewn together into strip sets. As a matter of personal preference, I press the seam allowance of each new strip as it is added, usually toward the darker fabric, unless the block construction dictates that it be done differently. After each strip set is pressed, place it squarely on the cutting mat. Align a horizontal line on your ruler with a seam line to square up the edge of the set and cut across the seams at measured intervals to create strip-set segments. Continue in this manner to make the required number of cuts.

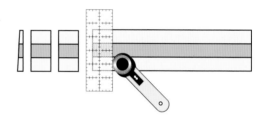

Strip piecing saves a tremendous amount of time and eliminates some of the steps that would be required to stitch individual pieces together one by one.

CHAIN PIECING

When you begin a project that requires you to join numerous identical pieces, chain piecing will speed the process and save an enormous amount of thread. Chain piecing simply means that you continue to feed pieces through your sewing machine one after another, without snipping the threads between each. After all the pieces have been sewn, cut the threads to separate them and press as instructed.

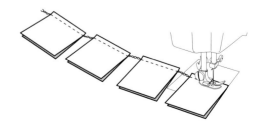

Pressing Seams

It's important to press your patchwork well so that the blocks fit together and lie flat when pieced into a quilt top. I use an iron on a hot, dry setting to press my pieces as follows:

1. Lay the patchwork on the ironing board, with the fabric you wish to press toward (usually the darker fabric) positioned on top. On the wrong side of the fabric, briefly bring the iron down onto the sewn seam to warm the fabric.

2. Lift the iron and fold the top fabric piece back to expose the front side of the seam. While the fabric is still warm, run your fingernail along the sewn thread line to relax the fibers at the fold.

3. Press the seam flat from the front side. The seam allowance will now lie under the fabric that was originally positioned on top.

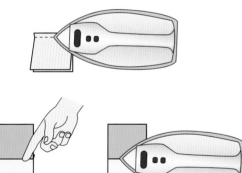

This method will help you achieve a finished block of accurate size, since less fabric is lost to the pressed fold of the seam allowance.

Pressing Triangle Units

Here is another quick but important pressing tip that works beautifully for me. Several patterns in this book instruct you to create triangles by layering a square with a drawn diagonal line on top of a second square or rectangle of fabric. After layering, the pair is stitched together on the drawn line, pressed, and trimmed. I recommend the following procedure when sewing and pressing these triangle units.

1. After stitching, open the top triangle and align its corner to the corner of the bottom piece of fabric to keep it square. Press in place.

2. Trim away the excess layers of fabric under the top triangle, leaving a ¼" seam allowance.

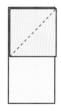 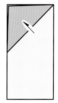 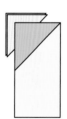

A common practice is to trim away the excess layers of fabric first and then press the triangle open, but I've found that for smaller-scale patchwork in particular, the pressing method outlined above is very reliable and results in fewer blocks that require squaring up later.

Pin Point

Direct Your Pressed Seams

When a pattern doesn't specify the direction to press your seam, consider the block construction before you consider the color placement. Pressing the seams in opposing directions will allow them to butt together when joined and produce accurate intersections. Whenever possible, press away from patchwork points and toward the side with the fewest seams.

COMPLETING THE QUILT TOP

The following sections cover the various steps needed to turn your beautiful blocks into a spectacular quilt.

QUILT-TOP ASSEMBLY

It's always a good practice to square up your blocks prior to assembling them into a quilt top. If the blocks are too small, double-check the seam allowance widths for accuracy and check your pressing to ensure that no excess fabric has been lost in the folds along the seam lines. Slightly trim outer edges on any blocks that are too large. Distorted or misshapen blocks can be lightly spritzed with spray starch, reshaped, and pressed to lie flat and square.

Lay out the finished blocks as instructed and evaluate the balance of color, repositioning them as necessary or even making substitutions to achieve the final look that you desire. To clearly define and anchor your quilt center, always position pieces or blocks with strong hues in the corners. To keep your blocks in their proper positions during assembly, I recommend using a water-soluble marker to lightly number each one in the seam allowance on the wrong side. Small adhesive labels can be numbered and affixed to the wrong side as a second option. I number from left to right with the row and block number. For example: 1-1, 1-2, 1-3, and 2-1, 2-2, and 2-3.

Normally, the seams of each row will be pressed in alternating directions so that they butt together when joined. For greater ease when assembling large tops, join the rows in groups of two or three. Next, join the grouped rows, working from each opposite end toward the middle, until you join the two halves.

BORDERS

When you are ready to add borders to your quilt, the following sections will walk you through the processes of sewing pieced, whole-cloth, and mitered borders to your quilt.

PIECED AND WHOLE-CLOTH BORDERS

Pieced borders are made by sewing several strips of fabric or pieced units together to achieve the proper length, while whole-cloth borders are cut from one piece of fabric. Pieced borders may require extra attention to accuracy to ensure that they fit the quilt center properly. Borders that are too long can appear ruffled, while borders that are too small can cause puckered areas in the quilt center. Also, all of the border measurements in this book are mathematically correct, but you may wish to adjust the length of whole-cloth border strips, particularly those cut parallel to the selvages (because there is little or no stretch to them), to ensure a proper fit. If you decide to adjust your strip lengths, cut them slightly longer than specified, and trim them to size later. Or, you can wait and measure your quilt top after it is complete, and then cut your strips to the exact length.

When joining border strips to the center of a quilt, I suggest that you fold each border piece in half to find the center, and then finger-press a crease. Next, fold each side of the quilt center and crease the midpoint. Line up the creases and pin in place for a perfect fit!

MITERED BORDERS

The measurements for mitered border strips in each quilt project include extra length to allow for the placement of the miters.

1. Crease the center point of the border strip and with right sides together, align it with the midpoint of the quilt top. Pin in place, with the excess border fabric extending beyond the quilt-top edges. Stitch the border to the quilt top, starting and stopping ¼" from each corner and backstitching. Repeat with the remaining borders.

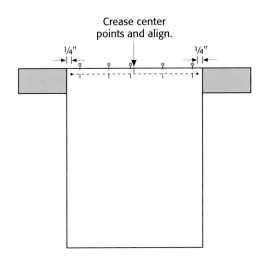

Crease center points and align.

¼" ¼"

2. With the wrong side up, lay the quilt top flat and overlap the border strips at one corner so that they cross at a 90° angle. Place a large acrylic ruler with a marked

45° angle line over the strips, positioning the ruler so that the 45° line is aligned with the edge of the border and the ruler's edge intersects the corner seam. Use a mechanical pencil to draw a line along the ruler edge where it lies across the border. Now place the bottom border strip on top and repeat the process. Prepare each corner in this manner.

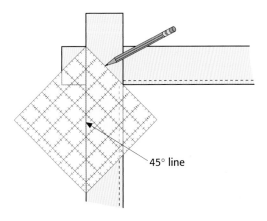

45° line

3. With right sides together, fold the quilt top and align the strips at one corner. Insert pins through the drawn lines of both strips to align them perfectly. Beginning at the inside corner, backstitch and sew the strips together exactly on the drawn lines to the outside edges. Lay the top down to check that the mitered seam lies flat. Trim away the excess fabric, leaving a ¼" seam allowance. Press the seam open. Repeat with the remaining corners.

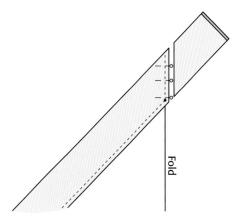

Fold

FINISHING TECHNIQUES

The topics that follow describe how your choice of batting can affect the appearance of your finished quilt and discuss the steps that I take when preparing projects for the quilting process. In addition, you'll find a review of quilting styles, as well as binding techniques—both standard binding and my unique method of mock bias-tape binding.

BATTING

There are many types of batting available for a variety of looks. Polyester batting ensures minimal shrinkage when washed and is a good choice for achieving a smooth, contemporary look. It can also be a good choice of batting if you favor prewashed fabrics, because the smaller degree of shrinkage will work best with preshrunk fabrics. If a softly puckered, old-fashioned look is more your style, you can combine thin cotton batting with cotton fabrics that haven't been prewashed, and immerse the finished quilt in water. Experiment to determine your preferences and always follow the manufacturer's instructions provided on the batting package.

BACKING

I cut and piece my quilt backings to be 3" to 4" larger on all sides than the quilt top. When you choose a backing fabric, remember that busy-looking prints will make your quilting less visible, while muted prints and solids will emphasize your stitches and quilting design. Also keep in mind that quilt tops with light-toned hues such as cream or muslin are best paired with similarly colored backings, because deep hues could result in shadowing or even affect the colors in your top.

The following examples illustrate ways that your quilt backings can be seamed to make the best use of your yardages.

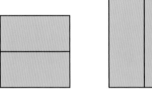

Lap quilts
up to 74" square

Twin-size bed quilts
up to 74" wide

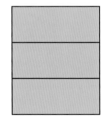

Full- and queen-size bed quilts
up to 90" wide

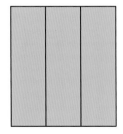

King-size bed quilts
up to 107" wide

BASTING

To prepare your quilt top for hand quilting, layer it with the batting and backing to form a quilt "sandwich," and then baste the layers together.

1. Place the backing fabric, wrong side up, on a large, flat surface. Smooth away any wrinkles and use masking tape to secure it in place.

2. Layer the batting over the secured backing fabric, centering it and smoothing away any wrinkles.

3. Center the quilt top over the first two layers and baste in place from corner to corner. Then baste vertically and horizontally at 3" to 4" intervals. I recommend using a long needle and white thread; colored thread might leave a residue of tinted fibers in the cloth of your quilt top.

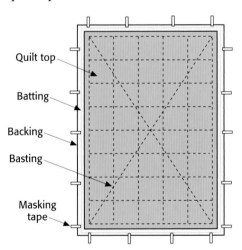

Quilt top
Batting
Backing
Basting
Masking tape

MARKING QUILTING DESIGNS

Quilt tops can be marked in many ways, depending upon the look you wish to achieve and the style of your quilt. If your quilt features appliqués that will be outlined, or if you plan to stitch in the ditch (along the seam line), it may not be necessary to mark the quilting pattern.

Pin Points

BASTING TIPS AND TRICKS

- I recommend stay stitching around the perimeter of any quilt with pieced borders to ensure that your seams remain intact during the basting and quilting process.
- If you intend to immerse your finished quilt in water, try basting the layers together with water-soluble thread. Once immersed, the basting stitches will vanish and you'll eliminate a step!
- When hand basting a quilt top, try threading your needle and placing the attached spool of thread in a mug or cup while you stitch. As you complete the sewing in each row, snip the thread at the spool and knot it, leaving a short tail. You'll always have the perfect length of thread, and the tail will enable you to easily remove the row of basting.
- If you have trouble getting down onto the floor to baste your quilt layers (or maybe you just plain don't like it), your machine quilter may be willing to handle this step for you, and the charge is usually minimal. It's money well spent!

Depending upon your preference, patchwork can be marked for outline quilting using ¼" masking tape. Grids or cross-hatching can be stitched onto background areas using various widths of masking tape as a guide. If you choose to use tape, remember to remove it at the end of each day to prevent any adhesive residue from adhering to the fabric. As a matter of personal preference, I use painter's low-stick masking tape when hand quilting lines on my projects. I find this tape to be very versatile because there are many widths available, the color is easy to see, and there is less adhesive.

More elaborate designs should be marked onto the quilt top using a quilter's

silver pencil or a fine-tipped water-soluble marker before the quilt sandwich is assembled. To ensure that the lines can be removed, always test your water-soluble marker on a fabric swatch before using.

QUILTING

There are many quilting methods to choose from. I personally love the look of hand quilting, but I don't always have the time needed to accomplish this for all of my projects. Frequently I have the background areas of my quilts machine quilted, with the appliqué and block areas left open for hand quilting. At first glance the quilt has the appearance of being completely hand stitched, although the actual hand quilting was done without a large investment of time.

Whichever method you choose, make sure your quilt is adequately quilted. After devoting the time and effort to assemble your quilt top, now is not the time to skimp! Beautiful quilting can elevate the status of even the simplest quilt, while the most striking quilt will suffer in appearance if the quilting is scant.

MACHINE QUILTING

For many of my quilts, I choose to have the top machine quilted in a swirling pattern that I created as an alternative to stippling. It's an excellent choice when I need an overall quilting design or filler for background areas. I've even had it quilted over the top of appliqué motifs with great results. This versatile design is easily sewn by stitching a free-form circle of any size, and then filling in the center with ever-reducing concentric circles (think cinnamon rolls!). When you arrive at the center of the circle, stitch a gentle wavy line to the next area you want to swirl and continue until your block or top is

A swirling pattern was machine quilted on "Calico Kaleidoscope" (see page 70).

complete. I think you'll find this quilting design to be the perfect choice for a variety of projects.

If you choose to machine quilt your project and would like additional detailed instructions, please refer to *Machine Quilting Made Easy!* (Martingale & Company, 1994) by Maurine Noble.

HAND QUILTING

If you prefer to hand quilt your project, place your quilt in a hoop or a frame and follow these steps:

1. Tie a knot in the end of a length of quilting thread approximately 18" long and insert the needle into the quilt top about 1" from where you wish to begin quilting.

2. Slide your needle through the batting and bring it up through the quilt top, gently tugging until the knot pops into the batting between the layers of fabric.

3. Make small, even stitches along the marked lines, taking care to stitch through all layers. Ideally, the distance between each stitch should be equal in length to that of your stitches. While your goal is to achieve tiny stitches, a consistent stitch size is most important.

4. As you near the end of your thread, make a knot about ⅛" from the quilt top and insert your needle, sliding it through the batting only. Bring the needle back up through the top, about 1" beyond your last stitch, tugging gently until the knot disappears below the cloth; carefully clip the thread.

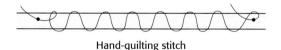

Hand-quilting stitch

BIG-STITCH QUILTING

Another charming style of hand quilting that I often use is the big-stitch method. It can be accomplished with or without the use of a hoop and will provide you with swift progress, since a stitch length of ⅛" to ¼" is very acceptable. Simply use a #5 embroidery needle with #8 pearl cotton to place a running stitch through the layers of the quilt sandwich. Begin and end your stitches as you would for traditional hand quilting.

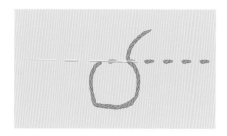

BINDING

The quilts in this book are bound with one of two methods: the traditional 2½" French-fold method or a mock bias-tape method that I use for most of my own quilts. The pattern directions provide yardage requirements and cutting instructions for binding based on using 2½"-wide strips cut on the straight of grain. The yardage will accommodate either method while providing enough binding to encircle the perimeter of the quilt plus approximately 10" to allow for miters at the corners.

TRADITIONAL FRENCH-FOLD BINDING

1. With right sides together, join the 2½"-wide strips end to end at right angles, stitching diagonally across the corners, to make one long strip. Trim the seam allowances to ¼" and press them open.

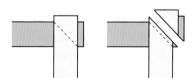

2. Cut one end at a 45° angle, turn it under ¼", and press in place. Fold the strip in half lengthwise with wrong sides together and press. If your quilt will include a hanging sleeve for display purposes, refer to "Making a Hanging Sleeve" on page 23 and add it prior to binding the quilt. The binding will enclose the raw edges of the sleeve.

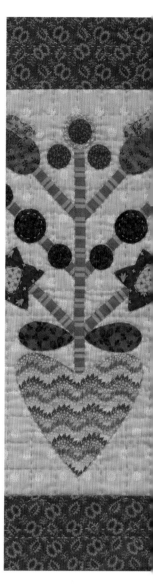

3. Beginning along one side of the quilt top, not a corner, use a ¼" seam to attach the binding, stitching along the raw edges. Stop sewing ¼" from the first corner and backstitch. Clip the thread and remove the quilt from under the presser foot.

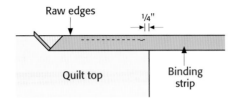

Raw edges

¼"

Quilt top

Binding strip

4. Make a fold in the binding, bringing it up and then back down onto itself to square the corner. Rotate the quilt 90° and reposition it under the presser foot. Resume sewing at the top corner edge of the quilt, continuing around the perimeter in this manner.

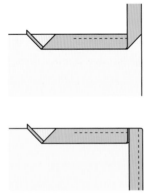

5. When you approach your starting point, cut the end at an angle 1" longer than needed and tuck it inside the sewn binding. Complete the stitching. The raw edges will be hidden within the binding.

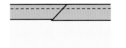

6. Bring the folded edge of the binding over to the back to cover the raw edges of the quilt. Use a blind stitch and matching thread to hand sew the binding in place. At each corner, fold the binding to form a miter and stitch in place.

MOCK BIAS-TAPE METHOD

For this method, you will need a bias-tape maker designed to produce 1"-wide, double-fold tape. For scrappy bindings that are pieced from assorted lengths of varying prints, I usually join the strips end to end using a straight seam and start with a straight rather than diagonal fold at the beginning. This results in a traditional look that I prefer for my quilts.

1. Cut your strips 2" wide and join them using a straight rather than diagonal seam.

2. Slide the pieced strip through the bias-tape maker, pressing the folds with a hot iron as they emerge from the tape maker.

NOTE: The seam allowances where the strips are joined will automatically be pressed flat to one side as the tape emerges from the tape maker.

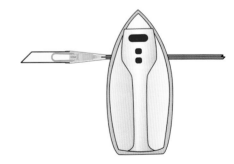

3. Open the fold of the strip along the top edge only. Turn the beginning raw end under ½" and press in place. Starting along one side of the quilt top, not at a corner, align the unfolded raw edge of the binding tape with the raw edge of the quilt, and stitch following the instructions in steps 3

and 4 of the French-fold method on page 22.

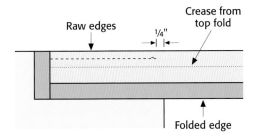

4. When you reach your starting point, cut the end to extend 1" beyond the folded edge and complete the machine stitching.

5. Bring the folded edge of the binding over to the back and hand stitch it in place as instructed in step 6 of the French-fold method on page 22. The raw end of the binding strip will now be hidden within the binding.

The mock bias-tape method of binding will result in a traditional look for the front of your quilt, while producing a wider width of binding on the back and providing extra color to frame the backing beautifully.

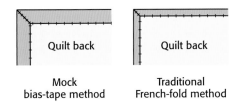

MAKING A HANGING SLEEVE

A hanging sleeve will provide the most efficient way of displaying your quilt on a wall, and it can be made from leftover quilt fabrics or muslin. It's easy to attach it as the binding is sewn to the quilt.

1. Cut a strip 8" wide and about 2" shorter than the width of your quilt. Fold the short ends under twice, measuring ¼" with each fold, and stitch.

2. Fold the strip in half lengthwise with wrong sides together. Center and baste it to the back of the quilt, positioning the raw edges so that they are flush with the top raw edge of the quilt. As the binding is stitched, the edges of the sleeve will become permanently attached.

3. After the binding has been stitched, use matching thread to blindstitch the bottom of the sleeve in place.

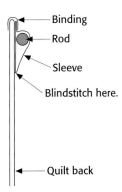

ATTACHING A QUILT LABEL

Remember to sign and date your quilt using a cloth label, and include any additional information you wish to share. To easily stabilize the cloth while you write, first iron a piece of freezer paper to the wrong side of the fabric. After the writing is complete, remove the paper. Press the raw edges under ¼" and baste or pin them in place. Use a small dot of basting glue in the seam allowance of each corner to anchor the label onto the backing, and then hand stitch it to the back of your quilt.

MACHINE APPLIQUÉ

In addition to standard sewing supplies for quiltmaking, you will need the tools and products listed below for the invisible machine-appliqué method featured in this book.

- **.004 monofilament thread.** Clear and smoke colors will accommodate any project.

- **Bias bars.** Use these plastic or metal bars of various widths when making appliqué stems and vines.

- **Embroidery scissors.** Make sure you have a pair of these small scissors with fine, sharp points for cutting cloth.

- **Fabric basting glue.** Use this water-soluble and acid-free glue in liquid form for basting stems and appliqué pieces.

- **Fabric glue stick.** This water-soluble and acid-free glue in stick form is great for preparing appliqué pieces.

- **Freezer paper.** Select any brand for use in making paper templates.

- **Iron.** You'll want a lightweight iron with a sharp pressing point, preferably with a nonstick surface, and/or a mini appliqué iron.

- **Open-toe presser foot.** This type of foot allows for better visibility while stitching.

- **Sewing machine.** Your machine should have an adjustable tension control and be capable of producing a tiny zigzag stitch.

- **Sewing-machine needles.** Use fine, sharp, size 75/11 quilting needles.

- **Stapler.** Use a standard stapler when preparing paper pattern pieces.

- **Staple puller.** You'll need this tool for removing staples from paper pattern pieces.

- **Tweezers.** Choose a pair with rounded tips.

PREPARING TO MACHINE APPLIQUÉ

When appliquéing by machine, you'll find that the preparation of template and pattern pieces is every bit as important as actually stitching the appliqués, and it can often be the lengthiest step of the process. The sections that follow will guide you through each step.

PREPARING MASTER TEMPLATES

As you prepare the templates for any given appliqué pattern, keep in mind that most shapes can be modified to fit your skill level if they appear too difficult. Simply "fatten" thin points and "plump" narrow inner curves. Your design will have essentially the same look, and no one will know but you.

1. Use a mechanical pencil to trace the pattern onto the paper (nonwaxy) side of a piece of freezer paper. Place a second piece of freezer paper under the drawn pattern with the waxy sides together, and pin in place.

2. Cut out the shape exactly on the drawn line and touch it with the tip of a hot iron to anchor the pieces together. Remove the pin, and finish fusing the paper pieces together with the iron. This will result in a sturdy template pattern that you can trace around to create your actual paper pattern pieces.

3. Mark any edge that does not need a seam allowance, such as a shape that is overlapped by another appliqué, with an *X*.

PREPARING PATTERN PIECES

Paper pattern pieces should always be cut exactly on the drawn lines because the seam allowance will be added when the shapes are cut from fabric. As you prepare your pattern pieces, take care to achieve smooth edges because the shape you trace and cut will be the shape that graces your quilt! An easy way to achieve smoothly cut edges is to move the paper, rather than the scissors, as you take long, smooth cutting strokes.

Use the prepared template to trace the specified number of pattern pieces onto the paper side of a piece of freezer paper. To save time when many pieces are needed, stack the freezer paper four to six pieces deep. Then pin or staple the layers, and cut several at once!

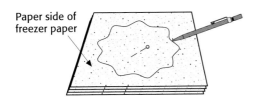

Paper side of freezer paper

Easily prepare mirror-image pieces by tracing the pattern onto one end of a strip of freezer paper, and then folding it accordion style before stapling (or pinning) and cutting. When you separate the pattern pieces, every other shape will be a mirror image.

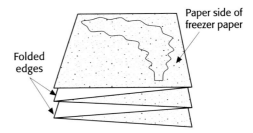

Paper side of freezer paper

Folded edges

PREPARING APPLIQUÉS

1. Apply a small amount of glue from a fabric glue stick to the paper side of each pattern piece and affix it to the wrong side of your fabric, leaving approximately ½" between each shape for seam allowances. Position each shape with the longest lines or curves on the diagonal, since bias edges are easier to manipulate than straight-grain edges.

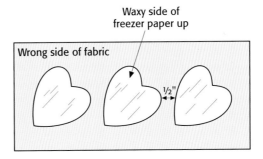

Waxy side of freezer paper up

Wrong side of fabric

½"

2. Cut out each shape, adding a scant ¼" seam allowance. Clip the seam allowance of all curves, both inner and outer, stopping two or three threads away from the paper to leave an intact fabric edge for pressing the seam allowance onto the waxy side of the pattern piece. The seam allowances at outer points do not require clipping, so an unclipped area of ½" or more leading up to each side of any point is just fine. Smaller and more pronounced

curves will need more clips while long, gently flowing curves will require fewer clips. Clip inner points, such as the one you find at the top of a heart shape, right to the pattern piece edge, taking care not to clip into the paper.

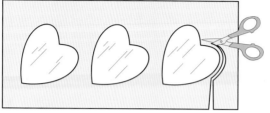

3. Working in a counterclockwise direction, use the point of a hot, dry iron to press the seam allowance over onto the waxy side of the pattern piece, beginning at a straight or gently curved edge. Always press the seam allowance toward the center of the shape because puckers or pleats can form along the edge of your appliqué if the seam allowance lies at an angle. The point of a seam ripper can be used to help you grab and manipulate the fabric when you work with small appliqué shapes. You'll find that overly enthusiastic pressing can cause the paper pattern piece edge to fold in upon itself and distort the shape of your appliqué, so take care! Continue pressing around the shape.

NOTE: If you are left-handed, you should work in a clockwise direction when pressing your seam allowances.

Stop each clip 2 or 3 threads from paper edge.

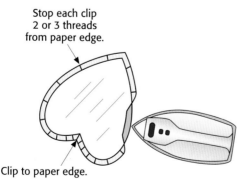

Clip to paper edge.

4. For sharp outer points, press the seam allowance so that the folded edge of the fabric extends beyond the first side of the pattern point.

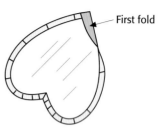

First fold

5. Fold over the seam allowance on the remaining side of the point and continue pressing. Apply a small amount of glue from the glue stick to the inside fold of cloth at the point (because fabric won't stick to fabric) and touch the cloth briefly with the point of a hot iron to fuse it in place. Use embroidery scissors to carefully trim away any seam allowance fabric that extends beyond the point.

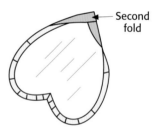

Second fold

6. To prepare an inner point, fold the seam allowance leading up to the point over and onto the waxy side of the pattern piece. Follow with the point of a hot iron in a sweeping motion to fuse the fabric in place.

NOTE: Handle the fabric at inner points sparingly, because it can fray easily. If fraying does occur, simply run your fingertip over the end of a fabric glue stick and gently smooth the loose threads over onto the pattern piece.

7. For the remaining side of the point, sweep the iron inward and away from the point to catch any stray threads while fusing the seam allowance fabric onto the waxy surface.

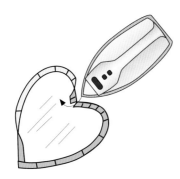

EVALUATING THE PREPARED APPLIQUÉS

Always turn your prepared appliqué over to the front and evaluate your pressing and preparation. If you do discover a flaw along the prepared edge of the appliqué, simply loosen the seam allowance where it has occurred and re-press it.

MAKING BIAS-TUBE STEMS AND VINES

To easily make smooth stems and vines, I like to use bias tubes. Bias tubes eliminate the need to press or turn under seam allowances, and the multiple fabric layers result in a stem or vine that is slightly dimensional. To make bias tubes, cut fabric strips the length and width specified in the project, and prepare the strips as follows:

1. With *wrong* sides together, fold the strip in half lengthwise and stitch a scant ¼" in from the long raw edges to form a tube. You may wish to trim the seam allowance of narrow tubes to ⅛"; this will allow them to be hidden under the finished stem.

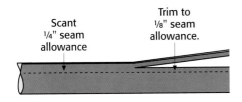

Scant ¼" seam allowance

Trim to ⅛" seam allowance.

2. Insert a bias bar into the tube and slide it along as you press the stem, making sure the seam is centered and lies flat.

Bias bar

3. This step is optional, but after removing the bias bar, as a matter of personal preference, I place small dots of liquid basting glue at approximately 1" intervals under the bottom layer of seam allowance. I then press the seam allowance with a hot iron to flatten and fuse it in place. I've found that gluing and pressing the tubes in this manner will keep the seams hidden, and it simplifies the process of laying out and stitching the appliqués.

You'll notice as you position the bias-tube vines and stems for each individual project that they often include just a little extra length. This gives you flexibility as you lay them out. Once you're satisfied with the placement of your stems and vines, trim away any length that you feel is not necessary.

PREPARING BACKGROUND FABRIC

I'd like to share a couple of steps that I take when preparing my background fabrics for the appliqué process.

- To reduce fraying and protect the seam allowance of your own background fabric, I recommend that you run a thin line of Fray Check around the perimeter of each block or border strip.

- Most of the appliqué patterns for blocks and borders in this book utilize creases for design placement. I call these "valley" creases, because the fold is directed inward to allow appliqué pieces to lie flat on the background fabric while you position them. In addition, these creases will enable you to repeat your design uniformly from

block to block. To prepare valley creases, fold the background fabric in half with right sides together and press a light crease along the center fold. Unfold the fabric, and then continue refolding and pressing to form vertical, horizontal, and diagonal creases.

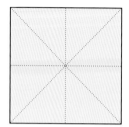

PREPARING YOUR SEWING MACHINE

1. Use a size 75/11 quilting needle in your sewing machine and thread it with monofilament. Keep in mind when selecting your monofilament color that you should match it to the appliqué print, not the background fabric. Generally, the smoke color will work best with medium and dark prints, while clear thread will work best with light or pastel hues. Wind the bobbin with standard neutral-colored thread or thread to match your background fabric.

2. Program your sewing machine to the zigzag stitch and adjust the stitch width and length until you achieve a very small stitch, as illustrated below. On my sewing machine, a width and length setting of one produces approximately 26 zigzag stitches to 1", measuring about $1/16$" wide—perfect! I also reduce the tension control to a level of one, because monofilament is very stretchy and if the tension setting is too tight, it can result in occasional bobbin threads becoming visible on the surface.

ΛΛΛΛΛΛΛΛΛΛΛΛΛΛΛΛΛ

Approximate stitch size

NOTE: After stitching, if a bobbin thread is visible on a dark appliqué, use a fine-tipped permanent marker in brown or black to place a tiny dot on the thread and it will disappear.

3. If an open-toe presser foot is available for your machine, substitute it for your machine's standard presser foot to allow you to see your stitching easily as you sew.

INVISIBLE MACHINE APPLIQUÉ

The following sections cover the actual appliqué process and provide you with detailed instructions for using your sewing machine to achieve truly invisible stitches. With a little practice, you'll find that this technique is easily mastered. If time constraints or even just a plain fear of the unknown have made you hesitant to make projects that contain appliqué designs, prepare to be surprised!

1. Before you begin stitching, lay out all of the prepared appliqué pieces on the background fabric to ensure that everything fits and is to your liking. You'll always work from the bottom layer to the top, so remove all but the bottom appliqués and secure them in place for stitching. This can be done with pins (taking care not to place them in the path of your stitching), or with liquid basting glue. If you choose to use glue, place tiny dots of the glue onto the cloth seam allowance of the appliqué at about $1/2$" intervals, and press it into place on the background fabric. Any glue that finds its way onto the paper can make the pattern piece difficult to remove, so be careful!

2. Direct the needle and bobbin threads toward the back of the sewing machine and position the prepared block so that the needle will pierce the background fabric next to the appliqué when it is lowered. Place your fingertip over the monofilament tail and hold it in place while your machine takes two or three locking stitches. If your machine does not offer a locking-stitch feature, reduce the stitch length to the shortest setting and take two or three small stitches in place.

NOTE: The placement of the first zigzag stitch can vary depending upon your model of sewing machine. If your particular model is designed to drop the first stitch inside the appliqué, then position your fabric accordingly.

3. Lift your fingertip from the monofilament and begin zigzag stitching so that the inner "zig" stitches land a couple of threads inside the appliqué, and the outer "zag" stitches drop into the background fabric exactly next to the appliqué. (As I stitch my appliqués, I have found that when I watch the outer "zag" stitches and keep them positioned correctly, the inner "zig" stitches will naturally fall into place.) After stitching a short distance, pause and carefully clip the monofilament tail close to the background but not so close that you risk cutting into the fabric.

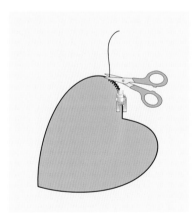

Stitch curved appliqué shapes at a slow to moderate speed to maintain a good level of control. Gently swivel the background fabric while you sew to keep the edge of the appliqué feeding straight toward the needle, or stop and pivot as often as needed to keep this angle of feed. You'll find that your speed will gradually increase as you feel more comfortable with this technique,

so don't worry about how fast or slow you stitch while you're learning.

4. To secure an inner point or corner, stitch to the position where the inner "zig" stitch lands exactly on the inner point of the appliqué, and stop. Pivot the background fabric so that the appliqué inner point is at a right angle to the needle, and the next stitch will pierce the background. For sharp or narrow inner points, you may wish to pivot and stitch twice to secure the appliqué well. Make sure the appliqué edge is aligned properly under the presser foot and continue stitching.

Stop and pivot.

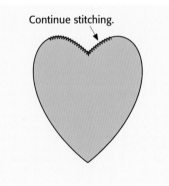

Continue stitching.

5. To secure an outer point or corner, stitch to the position where the outer "zag" stitch lands exactly outside the appliqué point and pierces the background fabric, and stop. Pivot the background so that the unsewn side of the appliqué is aligned to feed under the presser foot. As you begin to sew again, a second stitch will drop into the

ELIMINATE FRAYED APPLIQUÉ EDGES

When stitching appliqué designs that include overlapped stems or pattern pieces with unfinished edges, always make sure that the raw edges are tucked under the top piece approximately ¼" as you stitch them to the background fabric. This will result in a sturdy finished quilt and prevent frayed edges from appearing on your appliqués. If an unfinished appliqué edge has a seam allowance that is too scant after stitching, you can place a drop of Fray Check on the raw edge from the back to keep it from fraying.

For stem junctures that appear to have too scant an overlap, place a tiny dot of Fray Check on the front of the block at the point where the stems intersect.

point of the appliqué, often into your last stitch, securing it firmly to the background.

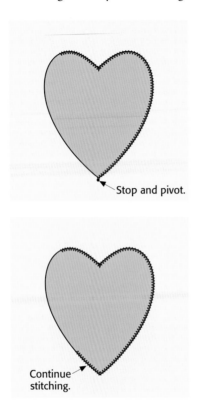

Stop and pivot.

Continue stitching.

6. Continue stitching around the perimeter of the appliqué until you are slightly beyond your starting point. End with a locking stitch, or take two or three straight stitches in place. Carefully clip the thread tails.

NOTE: You can place your locking stitches within the appliqué or on the background fabric. As a general rule, I position my stopping and starting points where the fabric's print will disguise them best.

STRING APPLIQUÉ

When there are two or more appliqués in close proximity, you can use a method I call "string appliqué" to speed the process and reduce thread waste.

1. Stitch your first appliqué as instructed in the previous section "Invisible Machine Appliqué," but instead of clipping the threads when you finish, lift the presser

foot and slide the background fabric to the next appliqué without lifting it from the sewing-machine surface. Lower the presser foot and resume stitching, remembering to begin and end with a locking stitch.

2. Remove the background fabric from the sewing machine after the cluster of appliqués have been stitched, and carefully clip the threads between each.

REMOVING PAPER PATTERN PIECES

1. On the wrong side of the background fabric, use embroidery scissors to carefully pinch and cut through the fabric near the center of the appliqué shape. Do not puncture the freezer paper or you run the risk of cutting through your appliqué. Trim away the background fabric, leaving a generous ¼" seam allowance to keep your appliqué secure.

2. Grasp the appliqué between the thumb and forefinger of one hand, and the appliqué seam allowance with the thumb and forefinger of your other hand; give a gentle but firm tug and the edge of the freezer-paper pattern piece will come free. Use the tip of your finger or the point of

a needle to loosen the remainder of the paper from the appliqué. Peel away the loosened paper and discard it. If any paper remains in the appliqué corners, use a pair of tweezers to carefully remove it. However, very small bits of paper that are too tiny to see or grasp easily are too small to worry about!

NOTE: It's not necessary to cut away the background of any piece that doesn't contain paper, such as a stem.

2. If necessary, place the completed block face down on your ironing board and lightly press from the back. Prolonged heat or high heat to the front of the block could weaken the monofilament and allow the appliqués to separate from the background fabric.

Practice Makes Perfect!

Before beginning your first project, I recommend experimenting with a couple of practice appliqués until you achieve the proper settings for your sewing machine and become comfortable with this method of appliqué. A heart-shaped practice pattern is provided below; it features gentle curves in addition to both inner and outer points.

I hope that you enjoy learning this fun and easily mastered method of appliqué!

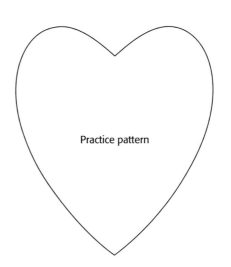

Practice pattern

Completing the Appliqué Process

1. Continue layering and stitching any additional appliqués until your block is complete. Keep in mind that you don't have to stitch any appliqué edges that will be overlapped by another piece, and remember to remove the paper pattern pieces between each layer.

Turn-Free Hand Appliqué

If you love hand needlework or just like the option of taking handwork with you when you're on the go, this section will provide you with some easy suggestions for preparing projects that are portable. Directions for the appliqué projects in this book will refer you to "Invisible Machine Appliqué" on page 28, but keep this technique in mind to give yourself added flexibility.

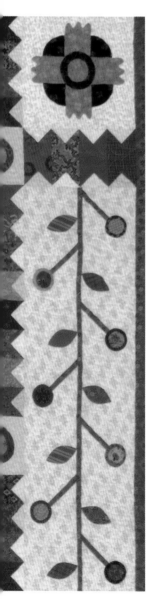

In addition to the supplies outlined in "Machine Appliqué" on page 24, you'll need the following items to hand stitch your appliqués:

- **Straw appliqué needles.** These are long, thin needles specifically used for hand appliqué. A size 9 or 10 needle works well for me, but ultimately you should choose a needle that you are comfortable using.

- **Thimble.** Choose a leather or metal thimble to comfortably fit your finger.

- **Thread.** Select high-quality, fine-gauge thread in a variety of colors to match your appliqués.

- **Plastic resealable bags.** Use clear plastic bags in the gallon size for toting your "in-progress" block and supplies.

Preparing Your Hand Appliqué

1. Referring to "Machine Appliqué" on page 24, prepare the appliqué pattern pieces and press valley creases into your background fabric to aid in positioning the appliqués.

2. Lay out the prepared appliqués on the background fabric to ensure that everything fits and is to your liking, and then remove all but the bottom pieces. For handwork that is truly portable, I recommend securing the appliqués to the background fabric using liquid basting glue rather than pins, as instructed in step 1 of "Invisible Machine Appliqué" on page 28.

3. Use pins or rubber bands to keep the remaining prepared appliqués together, grouping them separately by layers in the order that they'll be stitched onto your block.

Hand-Appliqué Stitch

Once your appliqués have been prepared, stitching them is a snap because the seam allowances are already turned under; no needle-turning is necessary. Use a resealable plastic bag to carry your block and easily see your supplies, and your hands will never be idle!

1. Cut a length of thread in a color to match your appliqué and insert one end of the thread through the eye of the needle. To tie a knot, form a small loop near the tail end of the thread, rolling it between your thumb and forefinger two or three times to draw the end through the opening. Pull the loop tight to form the knot.

2. Bring the needle up from the wrong side of the background fabric, just inside the appliqué, catching two or three threads along the appliqué edge. Pull the thread until the knot is flush with the fabric.

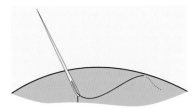

3. Insert the needle into the background fabric just behind the point where the thread exits the fabric, and come back up through the appliqué a tiny distance in front of your last stitch, again just catching the threads along the edge of the appliqué. Gently pull the thread until the stitch is secure. Continue stitching around the perimeter of the appliqué in this manner, taking tiny stitches to attach the appliqué securely to the background fabric.

NOTE: When I come to a point or corner in an appliqué shape, I place two stitches into it to ensure that it will be securely fastened to the background fabric.

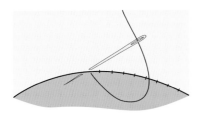

4. When you arrive back at your starting point, insert the needle and bring it out on the wrong side of the background fabric. Take a couple of small back stitches just inside the appliqué edge, drawing the thread through the loop each time to secure it and keep it well hidden under the appliqué. (Threads that are tied off under the background fabric can create a shadow effect through fine or light-hued fabrics.) Carefully clip the thread tail.

5. Referring to "Removing Paper Pattern Pieces" on page 30, gently remove the freezer paper. Again, it's not necessary to trim away the background of any piece that doesn't contain freezer paper, such as a stem.

This hand-appliqué stitch can be easily mastered with just a little practice, particularly when your seam allowances don't require turning. Keep in mind that for hand appliqué, as with machine appliqué, you'll always work from the bottom layer to the top. Remember to remove the paper pattern pieces before adding and stitching each new layer, and you can't go wrong!

Once you've completed your stitching and you're back in the comfort of your sewing room, lay the block face down onto a towel and lightly press it from the back.

QUAINT AND CHARMING

Whisper-soft plaids and ticking stripes invite you to sit for a moment and enfold yourself in quiet solitude. Settle in with your favorite book, and feel your cares melt away.

Finished quilt: 56½" x 62½"
Finished block: 6" x 6"

MATERIALS FOR LAP QUILT

Yardages are based on 42"-wide fabric.

- 2 yards of cranberry ticking stripe for border
- 1⅛ yards of tan print for blocks
- 28 squares, 6½" x 6½", cut from assorted scraps of homespun plaids and stripes for blocks
- 28 squares, 6½" x 6½", *cut on the bias* from assorted scraps of homespun plaids and stripes for blocks*
- 4 squares, 5" x 5", cut from assorted red homespun scraps for appliqués
- Assorted green plaid scraps for stem and leaf appliqués
- Assorted homespun scraps for appliqués
- Enough 2½"-wide random lengths of assorted homespuns to make a 248" length of binding
- 3½ yards of fabric for backing
- 63" x 69" piece of batting
- ⅜" bias bar

*Keep the bias-cut squares separate during the construction process for easy assembly when joining blocks for the quilt center.

CUTTING

All strips are cut across the width of the fabric unless otherwise noted. Refer to page 39 for the appliqué patterns and to "Machine Appliqué" on page 24 for pattern piece preparation.

From the tan print, cut:
- 14 strips, 2½" x 42"; crosscut into 224 squares, 2½" x 2½"

From the cranberry ticking stripe, cut:
- 2 strips, 7½" x 68", from the lengthwise grain
- 2 strips, 7½" x 62", from the lengthwise grain

From the assorted green plaid scraps, cut:
- 8 strips, 1½" x 17", for stems
- 16 *each* using patterns A, B, and C
- 8 using pattern E

From the assorted homespun scraps for appliqués, cut:
- 8 using pattern D
- 4 *each* using patterns F, H, and I

From *each* red homespun 5" square, cut:
- 1 using pattern G

PIECING THE SNOWBALL BLOCKS

1. Using a mechanical pencil, draw a diagonal line on the wrong side of each tan print 2½" square.

Quaint and Charming Lap Quilt

Designed, machine pieced, machine appliquéd, and hand quilted in the big-stitch method by Kim Diehl.

2. With right sides together, layer a prepared tan print square over two opposite corners of an assorted homespun 6½" square. Stitch the layered squares together exactly on the drawn lines. Press and trim as instructed in "Pressing Triangle Units" on page 15. Repeat for a total of 56 pieced squares.

NOTE: Exercise extra care when stitching the bias-cut squares to prevent the edges from stretching.

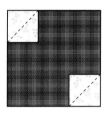 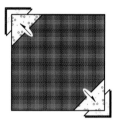

Make 56.

3. Repeat step 2, placing a prepared tan print square over the remaining two corners of each square. Repeat for a total of 56 Snowball blocks measuring 6½" square.

 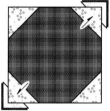

Make 56.

Pin Point

BOOK MAKEOVER

Consider having your favorite quilting books spiral-bound and the covers laminated at your local copy center. The cost is minimal, you'll extend the life of your books, and they'll lie perfectly flat as you follow directions and trace appliqué patterns.

ASSEMBLING THE QUILT CENTER

1. Lay out the Snowball blocks in eight horizontal rows of seven blocks, alternating the straight-of-grain blocks with the bias-cut blocks. Join the blocks in each row. Press the seam allowances of each row in alternating directions.

2. Join the rows. Press the seam allowances between each row open to reduce bulk along the seam lines.

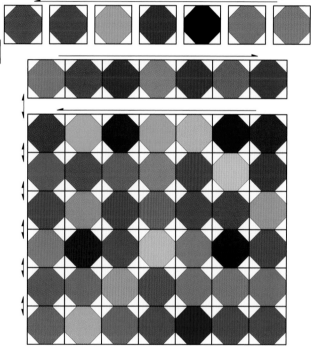

ADDING THE BORDERS

1. Referring to "Preparing Background Fabric" on page 27, press a center horizontal crease into each border strip of cranberry ticking stripe.

2. Referring to "Mitered Borders" on page 17, join a cranberry 7½" x 68" strip to the right and left sides of the quilt center, starting and stopping ¼" from each end. Press the seam allowances toward the cranberry strips.

3. In the same manner, join a cranberry 7½" x 62" strip to the top and bottom of the quilt center. Press the seam allowances toward the cranberry strips.

4. Sew the mitered corner seams. The finished quilt top should measure 56½" x 62½".

PREPARING THE APPLIQUÉS

Before beginning the appliqué process, I recommend applying a thin line of Fray Check around the perimeter of the quilt top to preserve the seam allowances.

1. Referring to "Machine Appliqué" on page 24, prepare the appliqué pieces.

2. Referring to "Making Bias-Tube Stems and Vines" on page 27, prepare the stems.

3. Using the pressed center creases on the borders for placement and beginning at the mitered seam line, position two prepared stems onto each border corner. Pin or baste in place. Referring to "Invisible Machine Appliqué" on page 28, stitch the stems onto the border.

4. Referring to the quilt photo, lay out the prepared A, B, C, D, and E appliqués, and pin or baste them in place. Stitch the appliqués to the border.

5. Continue adding and stitching the remaining appliqués, working in alphabetical order from the bottom layer to the top. Remember to remove the paper pattern pieces before adding each new layer.

COMPLETING THE QUILT

Refer to "Finishing Techniques" on page 18 for details as needed. Layer the quilt top, batting, and backing. Quilt the layers. The featured quilt was hand quilted in the big-stitch method with the Snowball block centers echo quilted at ¼" and 1" intervals. The tan print block corners were quilted with an intersecting pumpkin seed pattern. The borders were quilted along the ticking stripe lines, and the appliqués were outlined to emphasize their shapes. Join the 2½"-wide, random-length homespun strips into one length and use it to bind the quilt.

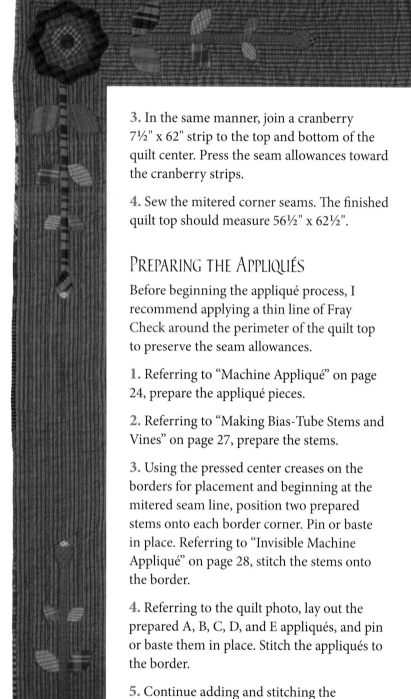

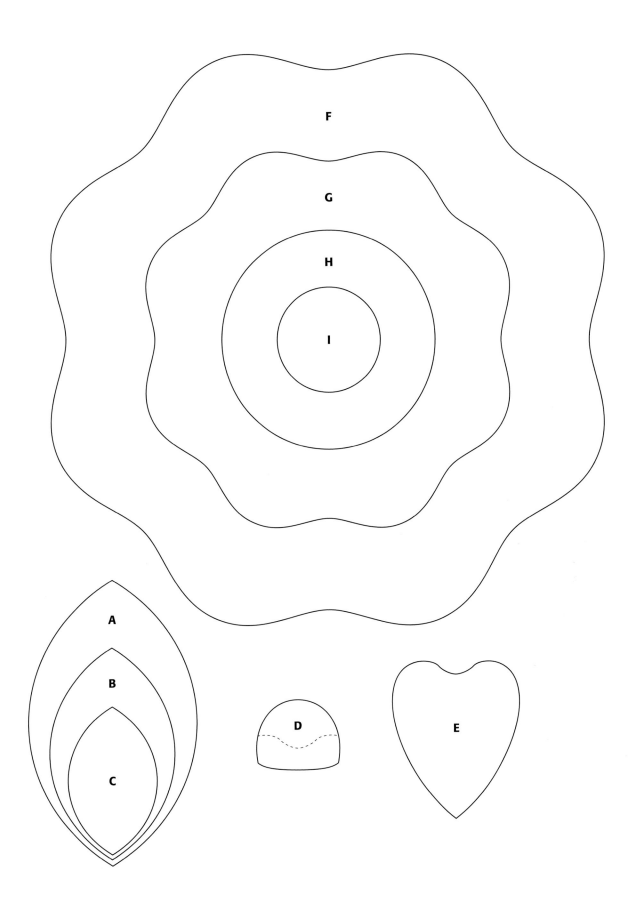

SHOOFLY POTPIE

Filled with unabashed charm and just a hint of spunk, this colorful little quilt embraces the prudent spirit of "making do."

Finished quilt: 19¼" x 23½"
Finished block: 3" x 3"

MATERIALS FOR DOLL QUILT

Yardages are based on 42"-wide fabric.

- 1 fat quarter of light print for inner border
- 1 fat quarter of dark red homespun for outer border
- 1 fat eighth or assorted scraps of dark blue homespun for border corner squares
- 6 assorted homespun squares, 3½" x 3½", for setting squares
- 5 assorted homespun squares, 5½" x 5½", for side setting triangles
- 2 assorted homespun squares, 3" x 3", for corner setting triangles
- Assorted medium and light print scraps for block backgrounds
- Assorted medium and dark print scraps for blocks and binding
- ¾ yard of fabric for backing
- 25" x 29" piece of batting

CUTTING

All strips are cut across the width of fabric unless otherwise indicated. One background print and one medium or dark print is used for each block. Please note that in keeping with the spirit of making do, the values for several blocks in this quilt have been reversed.

From the assorted medium and light print scraps for block backgrounds, cut:
- 24 squares, 1⅞" x 1⅞", in matching sets of 2; cut each square in half diagonally once to yield 48 triangles
- 48 squares, 1½" x 1½", in matching sets of 4

From the assorted medium and dark print scraps for blocks and binding, cut:
- 24 squares, 1⅞" x 1⅞", in matching sets of 2; cut each square in half diagonally once to yield 48 triangles
- 12 squares, 1½" x 1½"
- Enough 2½"-wide random lengths to make a 95" length of binding

From the assorted homespun squares, cut the:
- 5 squares, 5½" x 5½", twice diagonally to yield 20 side setting triangles; use only 2 triangles from each color
- 2 squares, 3" x 3", in half diagonally once to yield 4 corner setting triangles

From the fat quarter of light print, cut:
- 2 strips, 1" x 14¼"
- 2 strips, 1" x 17½"

From the fat quarter of dark red homespun, cut:
- 2 strips, 3" x 18½"
- 2 strips, 3" x 14¼"

From the fat eighth of dark blue homespun, cut:
- 4 squares, 3" x 3"; or substitute 4 squares cut from assorted look-alike blue scraps

Piecing the Shoofly Blocks

1. With right sides together, sew an assorted light or medium print triangle to a dark print triangle along the long side, taking care not to stretch the bias edges. Press the seam allowances toward the dark print. Trim away the dog-ear points. Repeat to make a total of four matching half-square-triangle units.

Make 4.

2. Lay out the four half-square-triangle units from step 1, four light or medium print 1½" squares of the same fabric, and one matching dark print 1½" square in three rows to form a block. Join the pieces in each row. Press the seam allowances toward the background print. Join the rows. Press the seam allowances toward the center row.

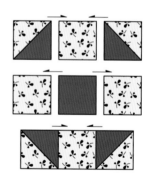

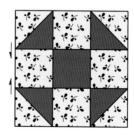

3. Repeat steps 1 and 2 to make a total of 12 Shoofly blocks measuring 3½" square.

Shoofly Potpie Doll Quilt

Designed, machine pieced, and hand quilted by Kim Diehl.

Assembling the Quilt Center

1. Lay out the 12 blocks on point with six 3½" setting squares, 10 side setting triangles cut from 5½" squares, and four corner setting triangles cut from the 3" squares as shown in the quilt diagram. Join the pieces in each diagonal row. Press the seam allowances toward the setting pieces.

2. Sew the pieced rows together and press the seam allowances in one direction. Add the two remaining corner setting triangles to the quilt center. Press the seam allowances toward the corner setting triangles.

Adding the Borders

1. Sew a light print 1" x 17½" strip to the right and left sides of the quilt center. Press the seam allowances toward the light print. Sew a light print 1" x 14¼" strip to the top and bottom. Press the seam allowances toward the light print.

2. Sew a dark red 3" x 18½" strip to the right and left sides of the quilt top. Press the seam allowances toward the red strips.

3. Sew a dark blue 3" square to each opposite end of the remaining dark red strips. Press the seam allowances toward the red strips. Sew these pieced strips to the top and bottom of the quilt center. The finished quilt top should measure 19¼" x 23½".

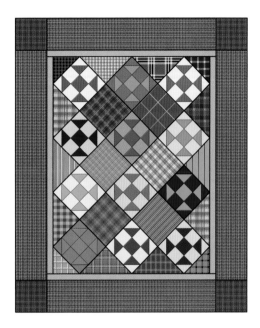

Completing the Quilt

Refer to "Finishing Techniques" on page 18 for details as needed. Layer the quilt top, batting, and backing. Quilt the layers. The featured quilt was hand quilted ¼" from the seams of the Shoofly blocks and in the ditch around the perimeter of each block. Selected lines of the homespun setting pieces were quilted for texture, and a fan pattern was stitched in the borders. Join the 2½"-wide, random-length strips into one length and use it to bind the quilt.

Pin Point

Scrappy Triangles without Waste

For scrappy setting triangles without waste, try this little trick. Cut the first square as instructed, and then use one of the triangles as a template for cutting the additional number of triangles needed from a variety of fabrics. You'll be able to incorporate more prints into your project and every triangle will be used!

Remembering Grandma

Preserve the softly spoken memories of days long past as you sew these classic blocks so reminiscent of your grandma's era. The timeless style of yesteryear will be yours to treasure when you stitch this quilt.

Finished quilt: 76½" x 95½"
Finished blocks: 15" x 15"

Materials for Bed Quilt

Yardages are based on 42"-wide fabric.

- 5½ yards of muslin* for blocks and border
- 3¾ yards of medium green print for blocks and border
- 2⅜ yards of red print for blocks and border
- 1⅜ yards of medium blue print for blocks and binding
- 5¾ yards of fabric for backing
- 83" x 102" piece of batting

For a finished quilt that will stand the test of time, be sure to select high-quality muslin.

Cutting

All strips are cut across the width of fabric unless otherwise noted. To make the best use of your yardages, please cut the pieces in the order given.

From the medium blue print, cut:
- 8 strips, 2⅜" x 42"; crosscut into 126 squares, 2⅜" x 2⅜". Cut each square in half diagonally once to yield 252 triangles.
- 9 strips, 2½" x 42" (binding)

From the muslin, cut:
- 8 strips, 2⅜" x 42"; crosscut into 126 squares, 2⅜" x 2⅜". Cut each square in half diagonally once to yield 252 triangles.
- 14 strips, 3½" x 42"; crosscut into:
  - 28 rectangles, 3½" x 9½"
  - 68 squares, 3½" x 3½"
- 11 strips, 1½" x 42"
- 5 strips, 3⅞" x 42"; crosscut into 48 squares, 3⅞" x 3⅞". Cut each square in half diagonally once to yield 96 triangles.
- 7 strips, 3" x 42"
- 27 strips, 2" x 42"

From the red print, cut:
- 13 strips, 1½" x 42"
- 27 strips, 2" x 42"

(continued on page 47)

Remembering Grandma Bed Quilt

Designed and machine pieced by Kim Diehl. Machine quilted by Celeste Freiberg.

From the medium green print, cut:

- 5 strips, 3⅞" x 42"; crosscut into 48 squares, 3⅞" x 3⅞". Cut each square in half diagonally once to yield 96 triangles.
- 2 strips, 2½" x 93½", from the lengthwise grain
- 2 strips, 2½" x 80½", from the lengthwise grain
- 1 strip, 2½" x 76½", from the lengthwise grain
- 2 strips, 2½" x 54½", from the lengthwise grain

From the remaining medium green print, cut:

- 152 squares, 3½" x 3½"
- 2 squares, 6½" x 6½"

Piecing the Pinwheel Blocks

1. With right sides together, layer a blue print 2⅜" triangle with a muslin 2⅜" triangle. Stitch the pair together along the long edge, taking care not to stretch the bias edges. Press the seam allowance toward the blue print. Trim away the dog-ear points. Repeat to make a total of 252 half-square-triangle units.

Make 252.

2. Lay out four half-square-triangle units to form a pinwheel. Join the pieces in each horizontal row. Press the seam allowances toward the blue print. Join the rows. Press the seam allowance to one side. Repeat to make a total of 63 pinwheel units measuring 3½" square.

Make 63.

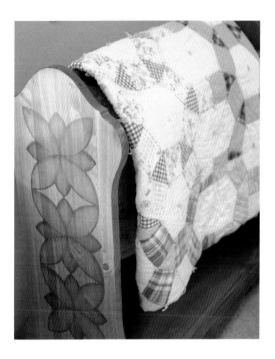

3. Lay out five pinwheel units and four muslin 3½" squares in three rows. Join the pieces in each horizontal row. Press the seam allowances toward the muslin squares. Join the rows to make a block unit. Repeat to make a total of seven block units.

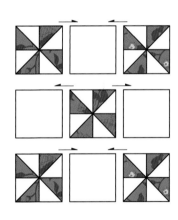

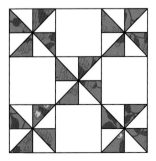

Make 7.

4. Lay out one block unit from step 3, four pinwheel units from step 2, and four muslin 3½" x 9½" rectangles to form a block. Join the pieces in each horizontal row. Press the seam allowances toward the muslin rectangles. Join the rows. Press the seam allowances away from the block center. Repeat to make a total of seven Pinwheel blocks measuring 15½" square.

Make 7.

Piecing the Geese in the Pond Blocks

1. Sew a muslin 1½" x 42" strip to each long side of a red print 1½" x 42" strip. Press the seam allowances toward the red print. Repeat to make three of strip set A. Cut the strip sets into 1½"-wide segments to yield 64 strip set A segments.

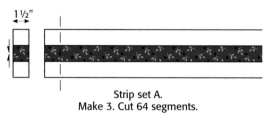

Strip set A.
Make 3. Cut 64 segments.

2. Sew a red print 1½" x 42" strip to each long side of a muslin 1½" x 42" strip. Press the seam allowances toward the red print. Repeat to make five of strip set B. Cut the strip sets into 1½"-wide segments to yield 32 strip set B segments measuring 1½" x 3½". Cut the remaining strip sets into 3½"-wide segments to yield 32 stripe segments measuring 3½" square.

Strip set B.
Make 5. Cut 32 segments, 1½" wide, and 32 segments, 3½" wide.

3. Lay out two strip set A segments with one 1½"-wide strip set B segment to form a nine-patch unit. Join the rows. Press the seam allowances toward the A segments. Repeat to make a total of 32 nine-patch units.

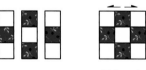

Make 32.

4. Lay out four nine-patch units, four stripe segments, and one muslin 3½" square in three rows. Join the pieces in each row. Press the seam allowances toward the stripe segments. Join the rows. Press the seam allowances away from the center row. Repeat to make a total of eight pieced block units.

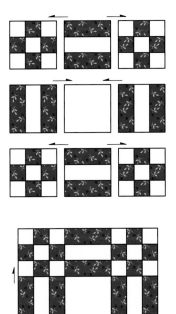

Make 8.

5. Layer a green print 3⅞" triangle with a muslin 3⅞" triangle. Stitch, press, and trim as instructed in step 1 of "Piecing the Pinwheel Blocks" on page 47. Repeat to make 96 half-square-triangle units.

6. Join a half-square-triangle unit from step 5 to two opposite sides of a muslin 3½" square. Press the seam allowances toward the muslin square. Repeat to make a total of 32 units.

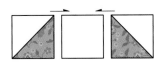

Make 32.

7. Join a half-square-triangle unit from step 5 to two opposite ends of a unit from step 6. Press the seam allowances toward the newly added pieces. Repeat to make a total of 16 units.

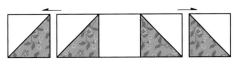

Make 16.

8. Join the units from steps 6 and 7 to a pieced block unit from step 4 as shown. Press the seam allowances away from the triangles. Repeat for a total of eight Geese in the Pond blocks measuring 15½" square.

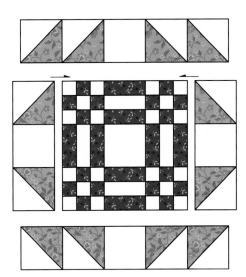

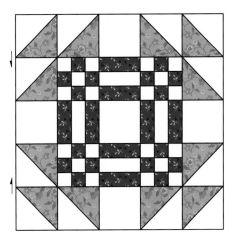

Make 8.

Assembling the Quilt Center

1. Lay out eight Geese in the Pond blocks and seven Pinwheel blocks in five rows as shown in the quilt diagram. Join the pieces in each horizontal row. Press the seam allowances toward the Pinwheel blocks. Join the rows. Press the seam allowances toward the rows with two Pinwheel blocks.

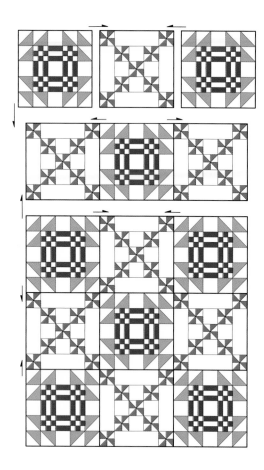

2. Join two muslin 3" x 42" strips end to end. Press the seam allowance to one side. Trim the strip length to 75½". Repeat for a total of two pieced strips measuring 75½" long.

3. Join three muslin 3" x 42" strips end to end. Press the seam allowances in one direction. Cut the strip into two 50½" lengths.

4. Join a 75½" strip from step 2 to the right and left sides of the quilt center. Press the

seam allowances toward the muslin strips. Join a 50½" strip from step 3 to the top and bottom of the quilt center. Press the seam allowances toward the muslin strips. The pieced quilt center should now measure 50½" x 80½".

Adding the Inner Border

1. Join a medium green print 2½" x 80½" strip to the right and left sides of the quilt top. Press the seam allowances toward the green print.

2. Join a green print 2½" x 54½" strip to the top and bottom of the quilt center. Press the seam allowances toward the green print.

Piecing the Checkerboard Segments

1. Lay out three red print 2" x 42" strips with three muslin 2" x 42" strips in alternating positions to form a strip set.

Join the strips. Press the seam allowances toward the red print. Repeat to make nine of strip set C.

2. Cut the strip sets into 2"-wide segments to yield 160 strip set C segments measuring 2" x 9½".

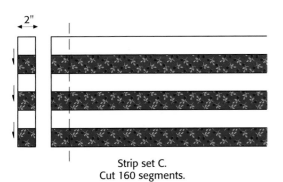

Strip set C.
Cut 160 segments.

PIECING AND ADDING THE RIGHT AND LEFT MIDDLE BORDERS

1. Using a mechanical pencil, draw a diagonal line on the wrong side of the medium green print 3½" squares.

2. Sew two C segments together as shown. Press the seam allowances to one side. Repeat for a total of 56 checkerboard segments. Reserve the remaining C segments for later use.

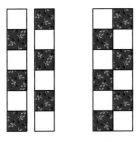

Make 56.

3. Referring to the illustration above right, lay a prepared green print square from step 1 over each opposite end of a checkerboard segment from step 2. Place the squares in mirror-image positions. Stitch through the squares exactly on the drawn lines.

Press and trim as instructed in "Pressing Triangle Units" on page 15. Repeat for a total of 56 pieced checkerboard segments.

Make 56.

4. Join two units from step 3 with the sawtooth points in mirror-image positions. Press the seam allowance to one side. Repeat for a total of 28 sawtooth units.

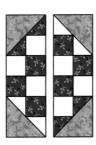 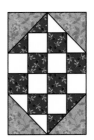

Make 28.

5. Lay out 14 sawtooth units to form a strip. Join the units. Press the seam allowances in one direction. Repeat for a total of two sawtooth strips.

Make 2.

6. Referring to the illustration for proper positioning, join a sawtooth strip to the right and left sides of the quilt top. Press the seam allowances toward the green print inner border.

Piecing and Adding the Bottom Middle Border

1. Referring to the illustration, join two reserved C segments. Press the seam allowance to one side. Repeat to make a total of 24 checkerboard segments.

 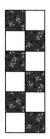

Make 24.

2. Referring to the illustration, align a prepared green print 3½" square over opposite ends of a checkerboard segment. Place the squares in mirror-image positions. Stitch, press, and trim. Repeat for a total of 18 units.

Make 18.

3. Join two units from step 2 as shown. Press the seam allowances to one side. Repeat for a total of nine sawtooth units.

Make 9.

4. Lay out the sawtooth units to form a strip. Join the units. Press the seam allowances to one side.

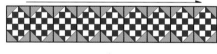

Make 1.

5. To make a corner square, join three checkerboard segments remaining from step 1. Press the seam allowances to one side. Referring to the illustration on the facing page, layer a prepared green print 3½" square over two opposite corners. Stitch, press, and trim. Repeat to make a

second checkerboard square, but sew the squares on the opposite corners.

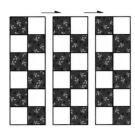

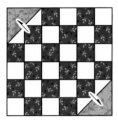 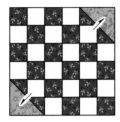

Make 1 of each.

6. Using a mechanical pencil, draw a diagonal line on the wrong side of each green print 6½" square. Referring to the illustration, align the square over one corner of each pieced checkerboard square as shown. Stitch, press, and trim.

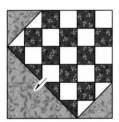 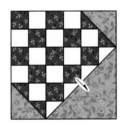

Make 1 of each.

7. Referring to the illustration, join a checkerboard unit to each short end of the sawtooth strip from step 4. Press the seam allowances toward the newly added units. Sew this strip to the bottom of the quilt. Press the seam allowances toward the green print inner border.

ADDING THE OUTER BORDER

Sew a medium green print 2½" x 93½" strip to the right and left sides of the quilt center. Press the seam allowances toward the green strips. Sew the green print 2½" x 76½" strip to the bottom edge of the quilt top. Press the seam allowance toward the green strip. The pieced quilt top should measure 76½" x 95½".

COMPLETING THE QUILT

Refer to "Finishing Techniques" on page 18 for details as needed. Layer the quilt top, batting, and backing. Quilt the layers. The featured quilt was machine quilted with diagonal lines placed over the checkerboard portions of the outer border and Geese in the Pond blocks. The triangle units in the blocks were outline quilted ¼" in from the seam lines. Feathered V shapes were quilted in the open background areas of the quilt center, and the remaining background areas were filled in with a stipple design. Feathered cables were stitched in the sawtooth portions of the border. Join the nine 2½"-wide blue print strips into one length and use it to bind the quilt.

54

Zinnia Basket

Capture the enchantment of an old-fashioned scatter garden with fabric flowers that never fade. These gently fluttering, sun-drenched blossoms will forever be a remembrance of summer, long after winter's snow has fallen.

Finished quilt: 62½" x 62½"

Materials for Lap Quilt

Yardages are based on 42"-wide fabric.

- 3 yards of cream print for blocks and borders
- 1¼ yards *total* of assorted medium prints in shades of blue, raspberry, pink, peach, cranberry, and butterscotch for appliqués and pieced border
- 1⅛ yards of apple green print for vines, appliqués, and first inner border
- ⅞ yard of cranberry print #1 for second inner border and binding
- ¾ yard of tan print for blocks
- ¼ yard of cranberry print #2 for appliqués
- ¼ yard of raspberry print for appliqués
- Scraps of assorted green prints for leaf appliqués
- 4 yards of fabric for backing
- 69" x 69" piece of batting
- ⅜" bias bar
- Liquid basting glue

Cutting

All strips are cut across the width of fabric unless otherwise noted. To make best use of your yardage, cut the pieces in the order given. Refer to pages 65–67 for the appliqué patterns and to "Machine Appliqué" on page 24 for pattern piece preparation.

From the cream print, cut:
- 2 strips, 1½" x 62½", from the lengthwise grain
- 2 strips, 1½" x 60½", from the lengthwise grain

From the remaining cream print, cut:
- 4 strips, 10½" x 32½"
- 1 rectangle, 16" x 29½"
- 1 strip, 3" x 29½"
- 2 rectangles, 7½" x 11"
- 2 rectangles, 4½" x 11"
- 2 squares, 7⅞" x 7⅞"; cut each square in half diagonally once to yield 4 triangles
- 2 squares, 6⅞" x 6⅞"; cut each square in half diagonally once to yield 4 triangles
- 8 rectangles, 3½" x 4½"
- 116 squares, 1½" x 1½"

From cream print scraps, cut:
- 56 using pattern D

From the tan print, cut:
- 1 strip, 8" x 42"; crosscut into 1 rectangle, 7½" x 22½", and 2 squares, 7⅞" x 7⅞". Cut each square in half diagonally once to yield 4 triangles.
- 1 strip, 4½" x 42"; crosscut into 1 rectangle, 4½" x 16½", and 4 squares, 3⅞" x 3⅞". Cut each square in half diagonally once to yield 8 triangles.

From the bias grain of the tan print, cut:
- 2 strips, 2½" x 16"
- 4 strips, 1½" x 13"

(continued on page 57)

ZINNIA BASKET LAP QUILT

Designed, machine pieced, and machine appliquéd by Kim Diehl.
Machine quilted by Kathy Ockerman.

From the raspberry print, cut:

- 8 *each* using patterns A and C
- 1 using pattern E
- 28 using pattern M
- 4 using pattern N

From cranberry print #2, cut:

- 8 using pattern B
- 22 using pattern D
- 1 using pattern F

From the assorted medium prints, cut:

- 56 squares, 4½" x 4½"
- 48 using pattern G, in matching sets of 3
- 16 using pattern H, in prints to coordinate with the G appliqué pieces
- 12 using pattern K

From the scraps of assorted green prints, cut:

- 43 using pattern I
- 36 using pattern J

From the apple green print, cut:

- 2 strips, 1" x 29½"
- 2 strips, 1" x 30½"
- 12 using pattern L

From the bias grain of the apple green print, cut:

- 4 strips, 1¼" x 14"
- 12 strips, 1¼" x 6"
- 12 strips, 1¼" x 4¾"
- Enough 1¼"-wide pieces to make 4 strips, each 68" in length

From cranberry print #1, cut:

- 2 strips, 1½" x 30½"
- 2 strips, 1½" x 32½"
- 7 strips, 2½" x 42" (binding)

Piecing the Center Basket Block

1. Align the ends of the two cream print 7½" x 11" rectangles with opposite ends of the tan print 7½" x 22½" rectangle at right angles as shown and with right sides together. Using a mechanical pencil, lightly draw a diagonal line on each cream print rectangle in mirror-image positions, beginning at the inner point and ending directly over the outside corner of the tan rectangle positioned underneath. Pin in place and sew the layers together exactly on the drawn lines. Press and trim, referring to "Pressing Triangle Units" on page 15. Press the seam allowances toward the cream print.

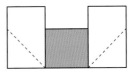

2. Join the two cream print 4½" x 11" rectangles to the tan print 4½" x 16½" rectangle as instructed in step 1, but draw the diagonal lines in the opposite directions.

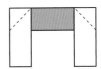

3. Lay out the pieced rectangles from steps 1 and 2 with the cream print 16" x 29½" rectangle and the cream print 3" x 29½" strip as shown to form the center Basket block. Join the rows, taking care to leave openings along the top edges of the basket where the handle will be positioned. Press the seam allowances toward the bottom of the basket. The pieced center Basket block should measure 29½" square.

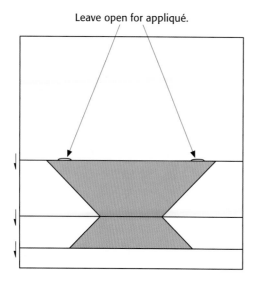

Leave open for appliqué.

APPLIQUÉING THE CENTER BASKET BLOCK

1. Cut an 18" x 18" square of freezer paper. Fold the square in half, then in fourths, and then fold it diagonally. Unfold the square and position a folded "wedge" over the large basket handle guide provided on page

65. Trace the curved line, refold the paper, and cut the shape out on the line. Align the center fold of the guide on the seam line along the top of the basket, and iron it in place. Use a water-soluble marker to trace the basket handle curve onto the cream print above the basket. Remove the guide.

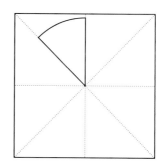

Trace handle curve on one "pie wedge." Refold and cut on drawn line.

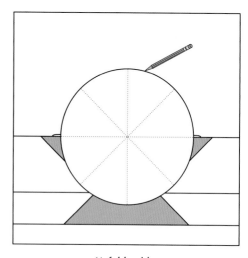

Unfold guide.
Line up fold with basket seam.
Trace handle curve.

2. Referring to "Machine Appliqué" on page 24, prepare each of the appliqué pieces.

3. Join the two tan print 2½" x 16" bias strips end to end. Press the seam allowance to one side. Referring to "Making Bias-Tube Stems and Vines" on page 27, prepare the basket handle for stitching. Place tiny dots of liquid basting glue along the drawn

handle line and press the prepared handle down onto the curve, centering it over the drawn line. Tuck the raw ends under the basket base through the openings in the seam, and stitch the handle to the block as instructed in "Invisible Machine Appliqué" on page 28. Sew the seam openings together.

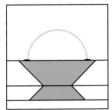 

Position handle over glue on drawn line, tucking raw ends into basket seam.

4. Lay out the prepared pattern E, positioning it approximately 1" above the basket base and centering it from right to left as shown. Use a water-soluble marker to trace around the shape, and then remove the pattern piece.

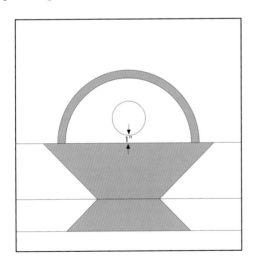

5. Prepare the bias strips cut from the apple green print; you will need the four 1¼" x 14" strips and four of the 1¼" x 6" strips. Place the inner raw ends of the long stems about ¼" from the drawn circle and position the

end of the short stems underneath the long stems as shown. Pin or baste the stems in place and stitch them to the background.

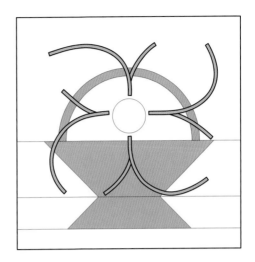

6. Lay out three prepared I appliqués as shown and stitch them to the background. Then position the eight prepared A appliqués, positioning them around the drawn circle and overlapping them into the circle approximately ¼". Pin or baste the petal appliqués in place and stitch them down. Remember to remove the paper pattern pieces after stitching the appliqués.

7. Position and stitch the eight B appliqués, aligning the raw edges of the petal bases with the A appliqués.

8. Lay out and stitch the eight C appliqués, staggering their placement with the first row of petals and again aligning them with the raw edges. In the same manner, add and stitch eight cranberry print D appliqués.

9. Add the E and F appliqués, stitching them in place to the completed center flower.

10. Arrange one H appliqué with three coordinating G appliqués at the end of each long stem, and then position the K and L bud appliqués along each short stem.

Work from the bottom layer to the top to stitch the appliqués in place, remembering to remove the paper pattern pieces between each layer.

11. Add 16 of the I appliqués and 8 of the J leaf appliqués to the stems, and stitch them in place. Then position 10 of the cranberry print D appliqués in a random manner along the stems. Stitch the appliqués in place.

ADDING THE INNER BORDERS

1. Join an apple green print 1" x 29½" strip to the right and left sides of the center Basket block. Press the seam allowances toward the green print. Sew an apple green print 1" x 30½" strip to the top and bottom of the center Basket block. Press the seam allowances toward the green print.

2. Join a cranberry print 1½" x 30½" strip to the right and left sides of the quilt top. Press the seam allowances toward the cranberry print. Join a cranberry print 1½" x 32½" strip to the top and bottom of the quilt top. Press the seam allowances toward the cranberry print.

Piecing and Appliquéing the Middle Border Basket Blocks

1. With right sides together, align a tan print 7⅞" triangle with a cream print 7⅞" triangle. Sew the layers together along the long side, taking care not to stretch the bias edges and leaving two ½" openings about 1" from either end to insert the basket handle. Press the seam allowance toward the tan print. Trim away the dog-ear points. Repeat for a total of four half-square-triangle units.

Make 4.

2. Using a 5" x 8" rectangle of freezer paper, trace the small basket handle/vine guide, including the dashed line, on page 66. Layer with a second piece of freezer paper, with waxy sides together, and pin in place. Cut the layers and fuse the pieces together to make a template.

3. Fold the template in half to find the center, and mark that position with an arrow. Fold a half-square-triangle unit in half and press a center crease. Position the dashed line of the guide along the seam allowance on the tan print, aligning center points. Trace the handle shape with a water-soluble marker and remove the template. Repeat for all four half-square-triangle units.

4. Prepare the four tan print 1½" x 13" bias strips to make bias-tube handles. Place tiny dots of liquid basting glue onto the marked handle line of a half-square-triangle unit and press a prepared handle in place, centering it over the drawn line and tucking the raw ends into the

seam openings. Stitch the handle in place. Sew the openings together in the center seam. Repeat to make four appliquéd half-square-triangle units.

5. Join a tan print 3⅞" triangle to one end of a cream print 3½" x 4½" rectangle. Press the seam allowance toward the tan print. Trim away the dog-ear points. In the same manner, join a second tan print 3⅞" triangle and cream print 3½" x 4½" rectangle to form a mirror-image basket base. Repeat to make a total of four pairs of basket base units.

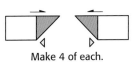

Make 4 of each.

6. Join a basket base unit to each tan side of an appliquéd half-square-triangle unit. Press the seam allowances toward the basket base units and trim away the dog-ear points. Repeat to make four units.

Make 4.

7. Join a cream print 6⅞" triangle to the bottom of each basket unit. Press the seam allowances toward the cream print. Trim away the dog-ear points. The pieced middle border Basket blocks should now measure 10½" square.

10½"

Make 4.

8. Lay out one prepared N appliqué, seven M appliqués, one D appliqué, and three J appliqués. Work from the bottom layer to the top to stitch the appliqués in place. Remember to remove the paper pattern pieces before adding each new layer. Leave one M appliqué unstitched on each side of

the Basket blocks to allow the vines to be inserted later. Repeat for a total of four appliquéd Basket blocks.

Make 4.

Appliquéing the Middle Border

1. Referring to "Preparing Background Fabric" on page 27, press a center vertical and horizontal crease onto each cream print 10½" x 32½" strip.

2. Beginning at the center of a prepared cream print strip, position the vine guide with the straight edge resting on the horizontal crease and the marked center arrow aligned with the vertical crease. Use a water-soluble marker to trace the curve of the vine onto the fabric. Flip the guide over to align with the opposite side of the crease; position the edge at the end of the first marked curve and trace the next curve. Continue flipping the guide and marking the curves in this manner, working from the center out to each opposite end. Repeat to mark the four border strips.

Center vertical crease

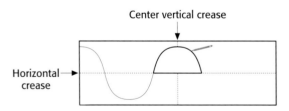

Horizontal crease

Use vine guide to draw vine curves onto border, working from center out to each end.

3. Prepare the remaining bias strips of the apple green print to make bias stems and vines. You will need 8 made from the 1¼" x 6" strips, 12 made from the 1¼" x 4¾" strips, and 4 from the 68" strips.

4. Place small dots of liquid basting glue along the marked line of a border strip; leave a small area free of glue at the crest of each curve to insert stems (refer to the diagram on page 64) and stop a few inches from each short edge to leave the seam allowances free for piecing. Beginning at one end of the strip, press a 68" length of prepared vine down onto the marked line, centering it over the line. Affix a 4¾" stem at the center point of each inner curve, tucking the raw end under the vine. Beginning and ending a few inches from each short edge, stitch the vine and stems in place. Make four vine-embellished border strips.

5. Working from the bottom layer to the top, stitch nine G appliqués, three H appliqués, and six I appliqués to each vine-embellished border.

6. Pin the unsewn portions of the vine to the background away from the seam allowance areas to keep them out of the way.

Adding the Middle Border and Completing the Appliqué

1. Join an appliquéd 10½" x 32½" middle-border strip to the right and left sides of the quilt top. Carefully press the seam allowances toward the cranberry print, taking care not to apply heat to the appliqués.

2. Join an appliquéd middle border Basket block to each end of the remaining border strips. Press the seam allowances toward the border strips, taking care not to apply heat to the appliqués. Join these strips to the top and bottom of the quilt top. Carefully press the seam allowances toward the cranberry print.

3. Unpin and position the remaining unstitched vines onto the borders, placing the raw ends where they will be covered by the M flower petal appliqués. Add a 1¼" x 6" stem to each side of the corner Basket blocks, tucking the raw ends under the longer vine where they meet. Finish stitching the vines, stems, and unstitched M appliqués.

4. Referring to the quilt photo on page 56, lay out and stitch four J appliqués, two K appliqués, and two L appliqués in each corner.

Piecing and Appliquéing the Outer Border

1. Using a mechanical pencil, draw a light diagonal line on the wrong side of the 116 cream print 1½" squares.

2. Align a prepared cream print square over two adjacent corners of an assorted medium print 4½" square, placing them in mirror-image positions. Stitch the layers together exactly on the drawn lines. Press and trim as instructed in "Pressing Triangle Units" on page 15. Make 56 units.

Make 56.

3. Fold each pieced 4½" square in half and finger-press a crease at the center position between the cream triangle corners. Set aside four squares for later use.

4. Carefully fold each prepared cream print D appliqué in half and finger-press a crease.

5. Align the crease of a D appliqué with the creased center of a pieced square, and use the crease to position the D appliqué about ¾" in from the raw edge. Pin or baste the appliqué in place and stitch it to the background. Repeat to make a total of 52 appliquéd squares.

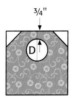

Make 52.

6. Using the four reserved 4½" pieced squares, stitch a prepared cream print 1½" square over a third corner of each. Press and trim as before. Center a cream print D appliqué over the middle pieced corner, about ½" in from the seam line. Stitch the appliqué in place. Make four corner squares.

Make 4.

Adding the Outer Border

1. Lay out 13 pieced and appliquéd 4½" squares from step 5 in "Piecing and Appliquéing the Outer Border." Join the pieces to form a border strip. Press the seam allowances in one direction. Repeat to make four.

Make 4.

2. Join a pieced border strip to the right and left sides of the quilt top. Press the seam allowances toward the middle border, taking care not to apply heat to the appliqués.

3. Join a 4½" square from step 6 in "Piecing and Appliquéing the Outer Border" to each end of the remaining border strips. Press the seam allowances toward the newly added squares. Join these pieced strips to the top and bottom of the quilt top, again taking care when pressing near the appliqués.

4. Join a cream print 1½" x 60½" strip to the right and left sides of the quilt top. Press the seam allowances toward the cream print. Join a cream print 1½" x 62½" strip to the top and bottom of the quilt top. Press the seam allowances toward the

cream print. The finished quilt top should measure 62½" square.

Completing the Quilt

Refer to "Finishing Techniques" on page 18 for details as needed. Layer the quilt top, batting, and backing. Quilt the layers. The featured quilt was machine quilted with a pebble design stitched in the background areas of the quilt center and outer border, and the background areas of the middle border were filled in with a small stipple. The basket bases were textured, and the large center flower was outlined to emphasize the appliqués. The picket fence squares in the outer border were quilted with an X shape. Join the seven cranberry print 2½" x 42" strips into one length and use it to bind the quilt.

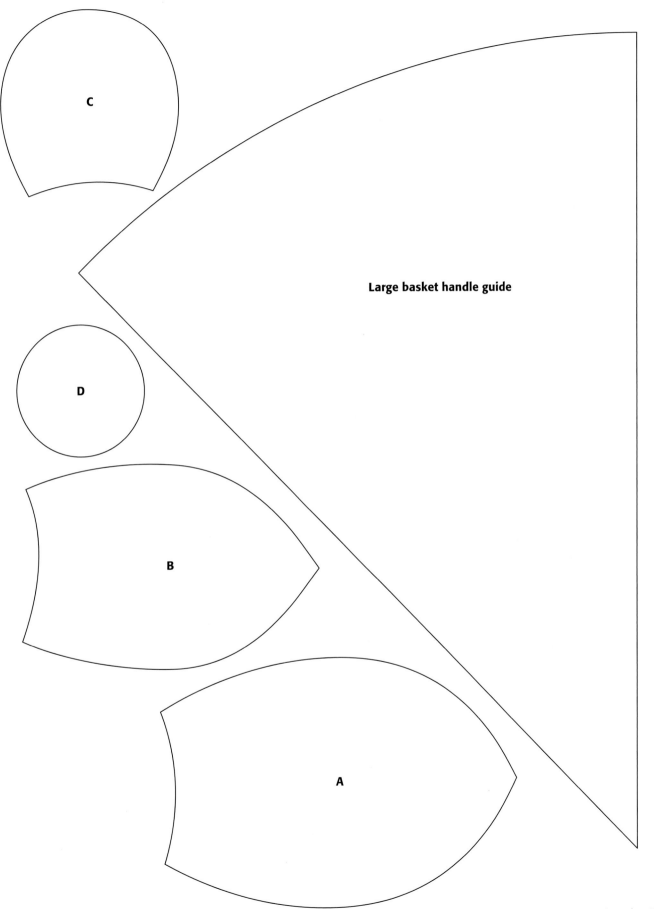

Large basket handle guide

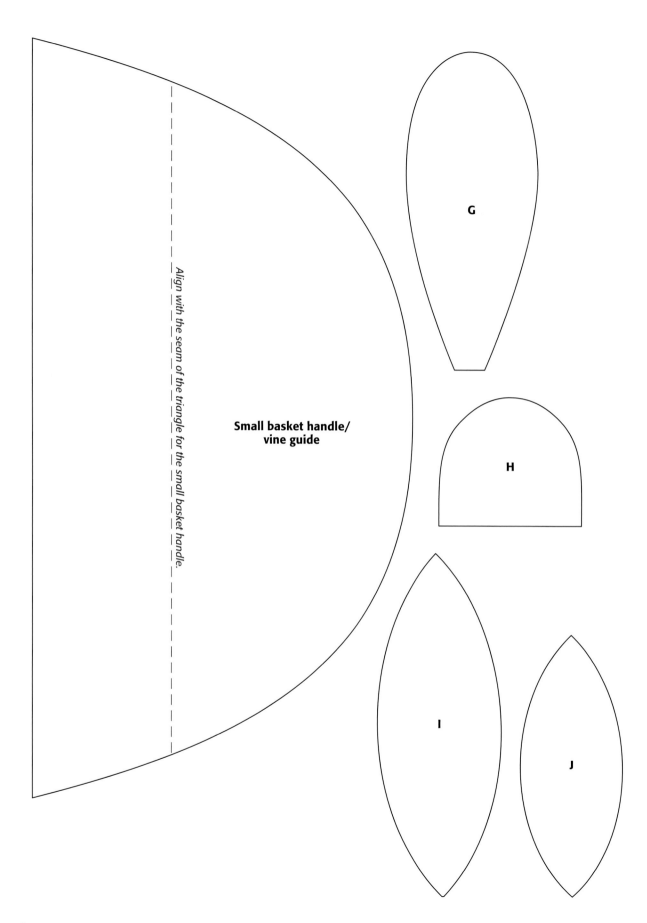

Align with the seam of the triangle for the small basket handle.

**Small basket handle/
vine guide**

G

H

I

J

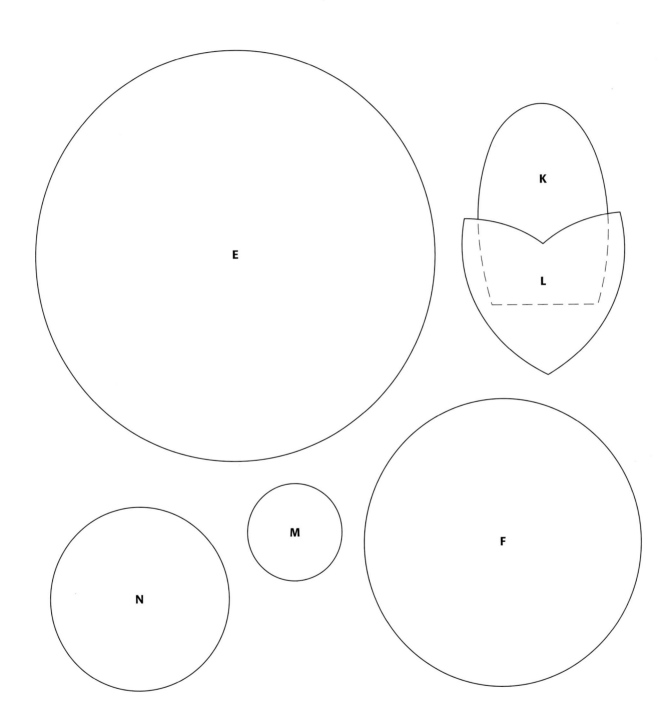

Calico Kaleidoscope

Revel in the allure of scrappy patchwork blocks as they seem to twirl and dance before your very eyes. This vibrant little quilt will infuse your room with prisms of color that will continue to sparkle for years to come.

Finished quilt: 44½" x 44½"
Finished block: 8" x 8"

Materials for Table Topper

Yardages are based on 42"-wide fabric.

- 1¾ yards of medium tan print for blocks and border
- 1⅝ yards *total* of assorted print fabrics for blocks and border
- ⅞ yard of brown print for blocks and binding
- ½ yard of light tan print for blocks and border
- 3 yards of fabric for backing
- 51" x 51" piece of batting

Cutting

All pieces are cut across the width of fabric unless otherwise specified. Please note that one assorted print is used for each block.

From 1 assorted print fabric, cut pieces for *1* block:
- 2 squares, 2⅞" x 2⅞"; cut each square in half diagonally once to yield 4 triangles
- 4 squares, 2½" x 2½"
  Repeat to cut pieces for a total of 16 blocks.

From the remaining assorted print scraps, cut:
- 136 rectangles, 1½" x 5½"

From the light tan print, cut:
- 3 strips, 2⅞" x 42"; crosscut into 32 squares, 2⅞" x 2⅞". Cut each square in half diagonally once to yield 64 triangles.
- 2 strips, 3" x 42"; crosscut into 16 squares, 3" x 3"

From the medium tan print, cut:
- 12 strips, 2½" x 42"; crosscut into 64 rectangles, 2½" x 4½", and 64 squares, 2½" x 2½"
- 15 strips, 1½" x 42"; crosscut into 16 rectangles, 1½" x 8½", and 272 squares, 1½" x 1½"
- 2 squares, 1⅞" x 1⅞"; cut each square in half diagonally once to yield 4 triangles

From the brown print, cut:
- 4 strips, 1½" x 42"; crosscut into 96 squares, 1½" x 1½"
- 1 strip, 5½" x 42"; crosscut into 4 squares, 5½" x 5½". From the remainder of the strip, cut 2 squares, 1⅞" x 1⅞". Cut each 1⅞" square in half diagonally once to yield 4 triangles.
- 5 strips, 2½" x 42" (binding)

Pin Point

Eliminate Snagged Threads

Change your sewing-machine needle as you begin each new project to prevent snagged threads from marring your block. If a pulled thread does become visible in the weave of the cloth, it can often be coaxed back into place by gently drawing your needle over it, from the outermost point back to the sewn seam.

CALICO KALEIDOSCOPE TABLE TOPPER

Designed and machine pieced by Kim Diehl. Machine quilted by Kathy Ockerman.

PIECING THE BLOCKS

1. With right sides together, join an assorted print 2⅞" triangle with a light tan print 2⅞" triangle, stitching the pair together along the long side and taking care not to stretch the bias edges. Press the seam allowance toward the assorted print. Trim away the dog-ear points. Repeat for a total of 64 half-square-triangle units.

Make 64.

2. Lay out four matching half-square-triangle units to form a pinwheel. Join the units in each horizontal row. Press the seam allowances toward the assorted print. Join the rows. Press the seam allowances to one side. Repeat for a total of 16 pinwheel units measuring 4½" square.

Make 16.

3. Using a mechanical pencil, draw a diagonal line on the wrong side of the 64 assorted print 2½" squares and the 96 brown print 1½" squares.

4. Layer a prepared assorted print square over the right-hand end of a medium tan print 2½" x 4½" rectangle. Sew the pair together exactly on the drawn line. Press and trim as instructed in "Pressing Triangle Units" on page 15. Repeat for a total of 64 pieced rectangles.

Make 64.

5. Layer a prepared brown print 1½" square over one corner of a 2½" medium tan square. Stitch, press, and trim as instructed in step 4. Repeat for a total of 64 pieced squares. Reserve the remaining brown print 1½" squares for later use.

Make 64.

6. Join a pieced rectangle from step 4 to two opposite sides of a pinwheel segment. Press the seam allowances toward the pinwheel. Repeat for a total of 16 pinwheel units.

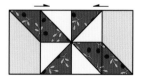

Make 16.

7. Join a pieced square from step 5 to each short end of the remaining pieced rectangles, placing them in mirror-image positions as shown. Press the seam allowances toward the pieced squares.

Make 32.

8. Join a rectangle unit from step 7 to each remaining edge of a matching print pinwheel unit. Press the seam allowances away from the block center. Repeat for a total of 16 Pinwheel blocks measuring 8½" square.

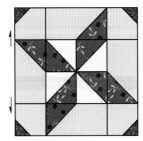

Make 16.

ASSEMBLING THE QUILT CENTER

1. Lay out the blocks in four rows of four blocks each. Join the blocks in each horizontal row. Press the seam allowances of each row in alternating directions. Join the rows. Press the seam allowances in one direction.

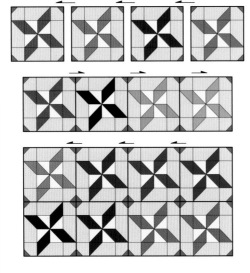

2. Layer a prepared brown print 1½" square over each short end of a medium tan print 1½" x 8½" rectangle, placing them in mirror-image positions. Stitch, press, and trim as instructed in step 4 of

"Piecing the Blocks" on page 71. Make 16 pieced rectangles.

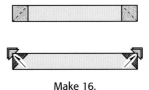

Make 16.

3. Join four pieced rectangles from step 2 to form a strip. Press the seam allowances to one side. Repeat for a total of four pieced strips. Join a pieced strip to the right and left sides of the quilt center. Press the seam allowances away from the quilt center.

Make 4.

4. Layer together a brown print and medium tan print 1⅞" triangle. Stitch, press, and trim as instructed in step 1 of "Piecing the Blocks." Repeat to make a total of four half-square-triangle units.

5. Join a half-square-triangle unit from step 4 to each end of the remaining pieced strips from step 3. Press the seam allowances toward the half-square-triangle units. Join these pieced strips to the top and bottom of the quilt center. Press the seam allowances away from the quilt center.

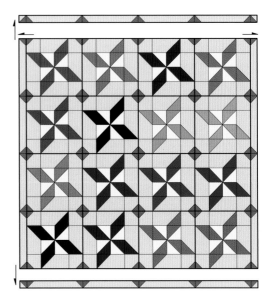

Piecing and Adding the Borders

1. Using a mechanical pencil, draw a diagonal line on the wrong side of the 272 medium tan print 1½" squares and the 16 light tan print 3" squares.

2. Layer a prepared tan print 1½" square over each short end of an assorted print 1½" x 5½" rectangle as shown. Stitch, press, and trim. Repeat for a total of 136 pieced rectangles.

Make 136.

3. Lay out 34 pieced rectangles from step 2. Join the pieces to form a pieced border strip. Press the seam allowances in one direction. Repeat for a total of four pieced border strips.

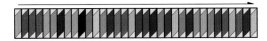

Make 4.

4. Join a pieced border strip to the right and left sides of the quilt top. Press the seam allowances toward the quilt center.

5. Layer a prepared light tan print 3" square over two opposite corners of a brown print 5½" square. Stitch, press, and trim. In the same manner, join a prepared light tan square to the remaining corners of the brown print square. Repeat for a total of four Square-in-a-Square blocks.

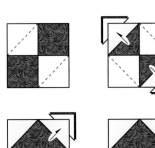

Make 4.

6. Join a Square-in-a-Square block to each short end of the remaining pieced border strips. Press the seam allowances toward the Square-in-a-Square blocks. Join these pieced strips to the top and bottom of the quilt top. Press the seam allowances toward the quilt center. The pieced quilt top should measure 44½" square.

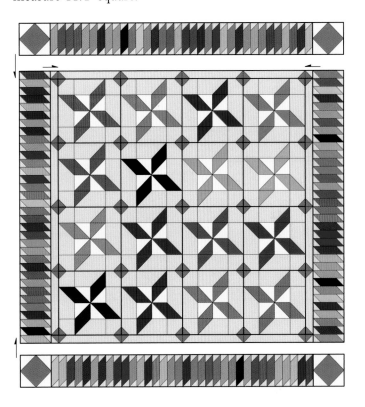

Completing the Quilt

Refer to "Finishing Techniques" on page 18 for details as needed. Layer the quilt top, batting, and backing. Quilt the layers. The featured quilt was machine quilted in an overall swirling pattern. A pattern and guidelines for duplicating this design are provided in "Machine Quilting" on page 20. Join the five brown print 2½" x 42" strips into one length and use it to bind the quilt.

A Tisket, a Tasket

Tradition abounds in these dainty little baskets brimming with gracious style and classic appeal, while the cherry-red prints and plaid create magic by adding a dash of unexpected spice.

Finished quilt: 37½" x 37½"
Finished block: 6" x 6"

Materials for Wall Quilt

Yardages are based on 42"-wide fabric.

- 1⅛ yards of medium blue floral print for blocks, outer border, and binding
- ⅔ yard of red plaid for inner border*
- ⅝ yard of ecru print for blocks
- ⅝ yard of tan floral print for setting blocks and triangles
- 1 fat quarter *each* of 3 assorted red prints for blocks
- 1¼ yards of fabric for backing
- 44" x 44" piece of batting

If you prefer to cut the inner border on the straight grain rather than the bias, ¼ yard is enough.

Cutting

All strips are cut across the width of fabric unless otherwise noted.

From the red print designated for the basket base, cut:
- 5 squares, 3⅞" x 3⅞"; cut each square in half diagonally once to yield 10 triangles. You will use only 9 triangles.
- 9 squares, 1⅞" x 1⅞"; cut each square in half diagonally once to yield 18 triangles

From the red print designated for the inner basket points, cut:
- 36 squares, 1½" x 1½"
- 9 squares, 1⅞" x 1⅞"; cut each square in half diagonally once to yield 18 triangles

From the red print designated for the outer basket points, cut:
- 72 squares, 1½" x 1½"

From the medium blue floral print, cut:
- 1 strip, 3⅞" x 42"; crosscut into 5 squares, 3⅞" x 3⅞". Cut each square in half diagonally once to yield 10 triangles. You will use only 9 triangles.
- 2 strips, 5½" x 27½"
- 2 strips, 5½" x 37½"
- 4 strips, 2½" x 42" (binding)

From the ecru print, cut:
- 9 strips, 1½" x 42"; crosscut into:
  - 54 rectangles, 1½" x 2½"
  - 27 squares, 1½" x 1½"
  - 18 rectangles, 1½" x 4½"
- 1 strip, 1⅞" x 42"; crosscut into 18 squares, 1⅞" x 1⅞". Cut each square in half diagonally once to yield 36 triangles.

From the tan floral print, cut:
- 1 strip, 6½" x 42"; crosscut into 4 squares, 6½" x 6½"
- 1 strip, 9¾" x 42"; crosscut into:
  - 2 squares, 9¾" x 9¾". Cut each square diagonally twice to yield 8 side setting triangles.
  - 2 squares, 5¼" x 5¼"; cut each square in half diagonally once to yield 4 corner setting triangles.

(continued on page 77)

Pin Point

STABILIZE BIAS STRIPS

When a project calls for working with lengths of fabric that are cut on the bias, here's a tip to help guard against stretching the delicate edges. Before cutting your strips, spray the fabric generously with starch and let it rest for a moment. Neatly lay out the damp fabric on your ironing board and press it flat with a hot, dry iron. This will help stabilize the cloth and there will be less chance of stretching during the cutting and piecing process.

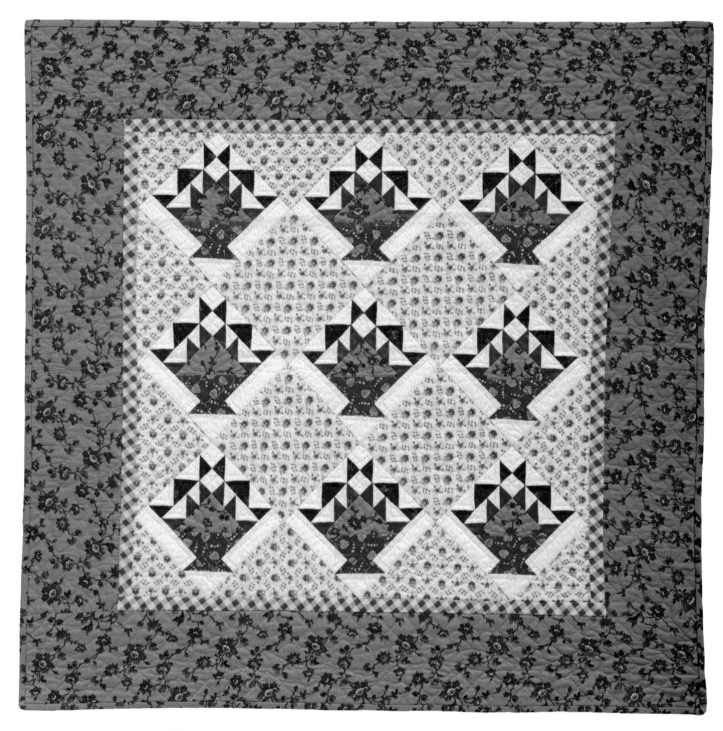

A Tisket, a Tasket Wall Quilt

Designed by Kim Diehl. Machine pieced and hand quilted by Barb Stommel.

From the red plaid, cut:
- 2 bias strips, 1¼" x 27½"*
- 2 bias strips, 1¼" x 26"*

If you've chosen to substitute a print for the red plaid, cut your strips across the width of the fabric.

Piecing the Basket Blocks

1. With right sides together, join a red print 3⅞" triangle with a medium blue print 3⅞" triangle, stitching the pair together on the long side and taking care not to stretch the bias edges. Press the seam allowance toward the red print. Trim away the dog-ear points. Make nine half-square-triangle units.

Make 9.

2. Using a mechanical pencil, draw a diagonal line on the wrong side of each assorted red print 1½" square.

3. Layer a prepared red print square for the inner basket points over one end of an ecru print 1½" x 2½" rectangle. Sew, press, and trim as instructed in "Pressing Triangle Units" on page 15. In the same manner, sew a prepared red print square to the remaining end of the rectangle. Press and trim. Repeat to make 18 pieced rectangles.

Make 18.

4. Join an ecru 1⅞" triangle with a red print 1⅞" triangle for inner basket points, stitching the pair together along the long side and taking care not to stretch the bias edges. Press the seams toward the red print. Trim away the dog-ear points. Repeat for a total of 18 half-square-triangle units.

5. Join a pieced rectangle unit from step 3 to a half-square-triangle unit from step 4 to form an inner-basket-point unit. Press the seam allowance toward the ecru print. Repeat to make nine units. With the remaining pieced rectangle units and half-square-triangle units, make nine mirror-image units.

Make 9 of each.

6. Join a unit from step 5 to the blue left-hand side of the basket unit. Press the seam allowance toward the blue print. Repeat to make nine units.

Make 9.

7. Join an ecru print 1½" square to the left-hand side of the mirror-image unit from step 5. Press the seam allowance toward the ecru print. Sew this unit to the remaining blue side of the basket unit. Press the seam allowance toward the blue print. Repeat to make nine units.

Make 9.

8. Layer a prepared red print square for the outer basket points over one end of an ecru print 1½" x 2½" rectangle. Sew, press, and trim. In the same manner, sew a red print square to the remaining end of the rectangle. Repeat to make 36 pieced rectangles.

Make 36.

9. Join the rectangle units from step 8 in pairs to form 18 outer-basket-point units as shown. Press the seam allowance in nine of them to the left; press the seam allowance in the remaining nine to the right.

Left-hand unit. Make 9. Right-hand unit. Make 9.

10. Join the nine outer-basket-point units pressed toward the left in step 9 to the left-hand side of the nine basket units. Press the seam allowance toward the outer-basket-point unit.

11. Join an ecru print 1½" square to the left side of the nine remaining units from step 9. Press the seam allowance toward the ecru print. Join this pieced unit to the side of the nine basket units as shown. Press the seam allowance toward the outer points.

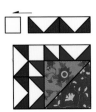

12. Join an ecru 1⅞" triangle to a red 1⅞" triangle for the basket base. Sew, press, and trim to make a half-square-triangle unit. Repeat to make 18 half-square-triangle units.

Make 18.

13. Join a half-square-triangle unit from step 12 to an ecru print 1½" x 4½" rectangle. Press the seam allowance toward the ecru print. Join this pieced rectangle unit to the bottom of the basket unit. Press the seam allowance toward the ecru print. Repeat for the nine basket units.

14. Join one ecru print 1½" square, one half-square-triangle unit from step 12, and one ecru print 1½" x 4½" rectangle as shown. Press the seam allowances in one direction toward the ecru rectangle. Join this unit to the remaining side of the basket unit as shown. Press the seam allowance toward the ecru print. Repeat to make nine blocks. The Basket blocks should measure 6½" square.

Make 9.

Assembling the Quilt Center

1. Lay out the nine Basket blocks on point with four tan floral print 6½" setting squares, eight side setting triangles, and two corner setting triangles as shown in the quilt diagram. Join the pieces in each diagonal row. Press the seam allowances toward the setting pieces.

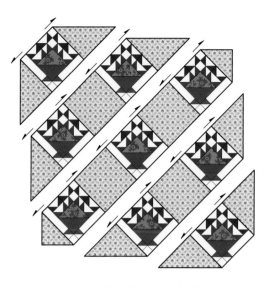

2. Join the rows, but do not add the upper-left and lower-right corner setting triangles yet. Press the seam allowances in one direction.

3. Sew the corner setting triangles to the quilt center. Press the seam allowances toward the triangles. Trim the seam allowance around the perimeter of the quilt center to ¼", if necessary. The pieced quilt center should now measure 26" square.

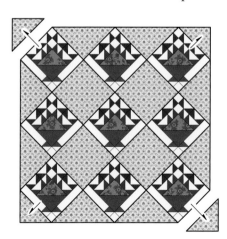

Adding the Borders

1. Sew a red plaid 1¼" x 26" strip to the right and left sides of the quilt center, taking care not to stretch the bias edges. Press the seam allowances toward the red plaid. Sew the red plaid 1¼" x 27½" strips to the top and bottom of the quilt center. Press the seam allowances toward the red plaid.

2. Sew a medium blue floral print 5½" x 27½" strip to the sides of the quilt top. Press the seam allowances toward the blue print. Join the 5½" x 37½" strips to the top and bottom of the quilt. Press the seam allowances toward the blue print. The quilt top should measure 37½" square.

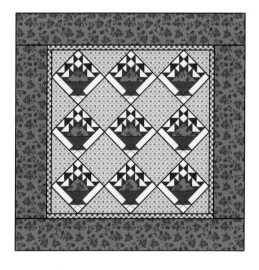

Completing the Quilt

Refer to "Finishing Techniques" on page 18 for details as needed. Layer the quilt top, batting, and backing. Quilt the layers. The featured quilt was hand quilted with a ¼" outline stitched around the basket bases and points, and on the inside of the points. A ¾" grid was stitched in each basket base, with a pumpkin seed pattern stitched in the open area above. The setting blocks were quilted with a feathered wreath design, and a coordinating feathered cable was stitched in the outer borders. Join the four blue floral 2½" x 42" strips into one length and use it to bind the quilt.

PLAIN AND SIMPLE

Pleasing jewel-tone prints and a generous measure of quilting elevate these otherwise ordinary patchwork blocks to entirely new heights. Plain meets pretty in this quilt that embodies simplicity itself.

Finished quilt: 81½" x 95½"
Finished block: 11" x 11"

MATERIALS FOR BED QUILT

Yardages are based on 42"-wide fabric.

- 8 yards *total* of assorted neutral prints for blocks, sashing, and borders
- 6½ yards *total* of assorted prints for blocks, sashing, outer border, and binding
- 7½ yards of fabric for backing
- 88" x 102" piece of batting

CUTTING

All strips are cut across the width of fabric unless otherwise indicated. Please note that each block contains four square-in-a-square units that are cut from one color, with the background for each square-in-a-square unit cut from a different neutral print.

From the assorted neutral prints, cut:

- 736 squares, 3" x 3", in matching sets of 4
- 82 strips, 1½" x 11½"
- 82 rectangles, 1½" x 2½"
- 35 squares, 1½" x 1½"
- Enough 5½"-wide random lengths (6" to 18") to make a 245" strip

From the assorted prints, cut:

- 140 squares, 5½" x 5½", and 140 rectangles, 1½" x 5½", in matching sets of 4
- 44 squares, 5½" x 5½"
- 89 squares, 1½" x 1½"
- Enough 2½"-wide random lengths to make a 368" length of binding

PIECING THE SQUARE-IN-A-SQUARE BLOCKS

1. Using a mechanical pencil, draw a diagonal line on the wrong side of each neutral print 3" square.

2. With right sides together, layer a prepared neutral print square over two opposite corners of an assorted print 5½" square. Stitch the layered squares together exactly on the drawn lines. Press and trim as instructed in "Pressing Triangle Units" on page 15. Repeat for a total of 184 pieced square units.

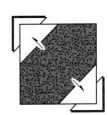

Make 184.

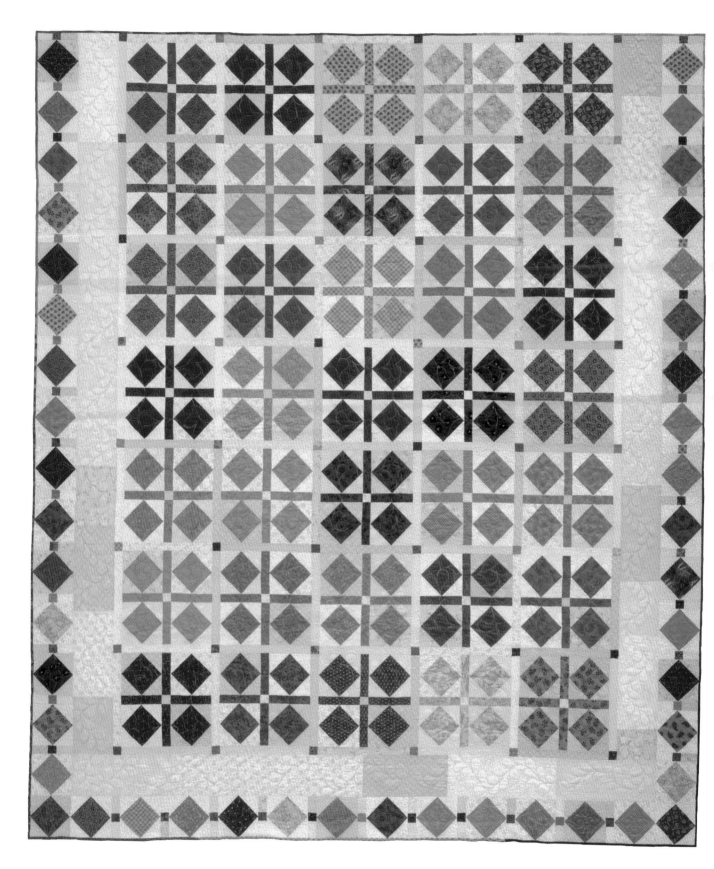

PLAIN AND SIMPLE BED QUILT

Designed by Kim Diehl. Machine pieced by Terry Anderson, Donna Clayson, Kim Diehl, and Deslynn Mecham. Machine quilted by Kathy Ockerman.

3. Repeat step 2, placing a prepared neutral print 3" square over the remaining two corners of each pieced square unit. Repeat for a total of 184 square-in-a-square units.

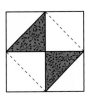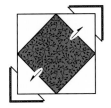

Make 184.

4. Lay out four matching units from step 3, four matching print 1½" x 5½" rectangles, and one neutral print 1½" square to form a Square-in-a-Square block. Join the pieces in each horizontal row and press toward the sashing. Join the rows. Press the seam allowances toward the center sashing row. Repeat to form a total of 35 Square-in-a-Square blocks measuring 11½" square. Reserve the remaining 44 square-in-a-square units for use in the outer border.

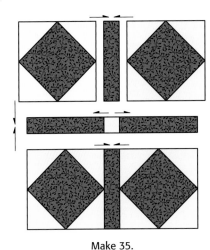

Make 35.

ASSEMBLING THE QUILT CENTER

1. Lay out six assorted print 1½" squares and five assorted neutral print 1½" x 11½" strips in alternating positions. Join to form a sashing row. Press the seam allowances

toward the neutral print. Repeat for a total of eight sashing rows.

Make 8.

2. Lay out six neutral print 1½" x 11½" strips and five Square-in-a-Square blocks in alternating positions. Join to form a block row. Press the seam allowances toward the neutral strips. Repeat for a total of seven block rows.

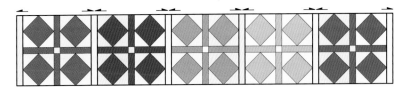

Make 7.

3. Lay out the sashing rows from step 1 and the block rows from step 2 in alternating positions. Join the rows. Press the seam allowances toward the sashing rows. The pieced quilt center should now measure 61½" x 85½".

ADDING THE PIECED BORDERS

1. Sew the 5½"-wide, random-length neutral print pieces together to make a strip at least 245" long. Cut the strip into two strips 85½" long and one strip 71½" long.

2. Sew an 85½"-long inner-border strip to the right and left sides of the quilt center. Press the seam allowances toward the border strips. Join the 71½"-long border strip to the bottom edge of the quilt center. Press the seam allowance toward the border.

3. Sew a neutral print 1½" x 2½" rectangle to two opposite sides of an assorted print 1½" square. Press the seam allowances toward the neutral print. Repeat for a total of 41 rectangle units.

Make 41.

4. Lay out 15 rectangle units from step 3 and 15 reserved square-in-a-square units in alternating positions. Join the units to form an outer-border strip. Press the seam allowances toward the rectangle units. Repeat to make two side outer-border strips.

Make 2.

5. Repeat step 4 using 11 rectangle units from step 3 and 12 reserved square-in-a-square units. Add a reserved square-in-a-square unit to each short end of the pieced outer-border strip. Press the seam allowances to one side.

Make 1.

6. Join an outer-border strip from step 4 to the right and left sides of the quilt top. Press the seam allowances toward the neutral inner border. Join the remaining outer-border strip to the bottom edge of the quilt top. Press the seam allowances toward the neutral inner border. The pieced quilt top should measure 81½" x 95½".

COMPLETING THE QUILT

Refer to "Finishing Techniques" on page 18 for details as needed. Layer the quilt top, batting, and backing. Quilt the layers. The featured quilt was machine quilted with a feathered wreath design in the blocks and a serpentine feathered cable stitched in the neutral borders. The remaining background areas were filled in with a small-scale stipple. Join the 2½"-wide, random-length strips into one length and use it to bind the quilt.

Pin Point

SIMPLE STITCH REMOVAL

When "un-sewing" a seam, a clean eraser or the sticky side of a length of masking tape can be lightly rubbed over any remaining threads to loosen and remove them from the cloth.

IDAHO FARM GIRL

Awash with color and soft as a gentle rain, this quilt blooms with all the modest charm of a farmhouse garden. Wrap yourself in warmth and sit a spell as the virtues of country living soothe your soul.

Finished quilt: 65½" x 65½"
Finished blocks: 5" x 5"

MATERIALS FOR LAP QUILT

Yardages are based on 42"-wide fabric.

- 3½ yards *total* of assorted cream prints for block backgrounds
- 3⅛ yards *total* of assorted light, medium, and dark prints for blocks
- 2 yards *total* of assorted red prints for blocks and binding
- 4 yards of fabric for backing
- 72" x 72" piece of batting

CUTTING

All strips are cut across the width of fabric unless otherwise noted. To simplify the process, cutting instructions are provided separately for each type of block. Depending upon the number of prints you have on hand, you may wish to cut more than one set from some of the assorted light, medium, and dark prints, and the assorted red prints as well, to produce the required number of pieces. The assorted cream background prints are used randomly within each block for a scrappy "make do" look.

SNOWBALL VARIATION BLOCK

From the assorted cream prints, cut:
- 864 squares, 1½" x 1½"

From the assorted light, medium, and dark prints, cut:
- 432 squares, 3" x 3", in matching sets of 4

FARMER'S DAUGHTER BLOCK

From the assorted red prints, cut:
- 793 squares, 1½" x 1½", in matching sets of 13 squares

From the assorted cream prints, cut:
- 488 squares, 1½" x 1½"
- 244 rectangles, 1½" x 3½"

BINDING

From the assorted red prints, cut:
- Enough 2½"-wide random lengths to make a 272" length of binding

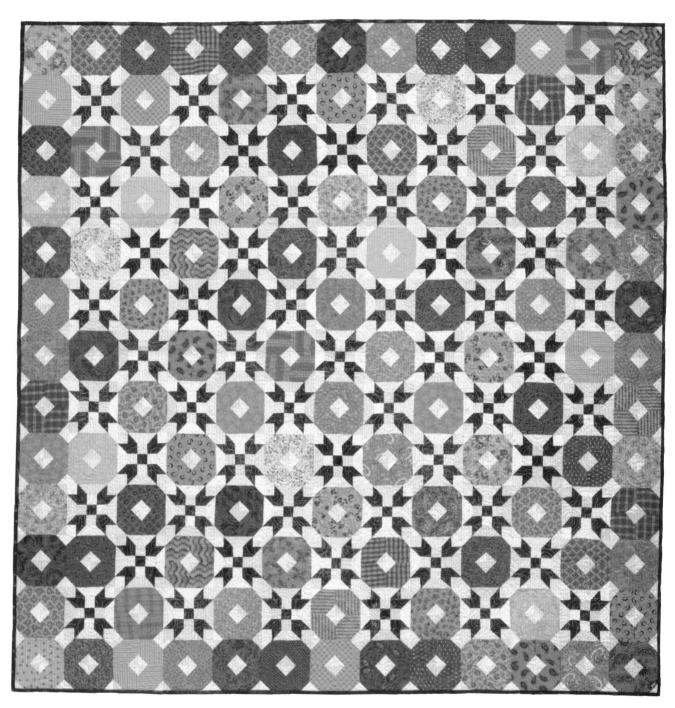

Idaho Farm Girl Lap Quilt

Designed by Kim Diehl. Machine pieced by Evelyne Schow. Machine quilted by Kathy Ockerman.

PIECING THE SNOWBALL VARIATION BLOCKS

1. Using a mechanical pencil, draw a diagonal line on the wrong side of the 864 assorted cream print 1½" background squares.

2. Select one set of four matching 3" squares. With right sides together, layer a prepared 1½" background square over one corner of each 3" square in the set. Referring to "Chain Piecing" on page 14, stitch each layered pair together exactly on the drawn line.

Make 4.

3. Repeat step 2, placing a prepared 1½" background square on the opposite corner of each 3" square.

Make 4.

4. Press and trim the pieced units from step 3 as instructed in "Pressing Triangle Units" on page 15.

Make 4.

5. Lay out the pieced units in two horizontal rows to form a Snowball Variation block. Join the pieces in each row. Press the seam allowances in opposite directions. Join the block halves. Press the seam allowances open.

6. Repeat steps 2 through 5 using the remaining sets of 3" light, medium, and dark print squares for a total of 108 Snowball Variation blocks measuring 5½" square.

PIECING THE FARMER'S DAUGHTER BLOCKS

1. Select one set of 13 matching red print 1½" squares. Lay out five red print squares and four 1½" cream print squares in three horizontal rows to form a nine-patch unit. Join the pieces in each row. Press the seam allowances toward the red print. Join the rows. Press the seam allowances away from the center row.

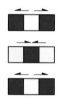

2. Draw a diagonal line on the wrong side of the eight remaining red print 1½" squares.

3. With right sides together, align a prepared red print square on each opposite end of a cream print 1½" x 3½" rectangle, placing them in mirror-image positions. Sew the layers together exactly on the drawn lines. Press and trim as instructed in "Pressing Triangle Units" on page 15. Repeat for a total of four units.

Make 4.

4. Join a unit from step 3 to two opposite sides of the nine-patch unit. Press the seam allowances toward the nine-patch unit.

5. Sew a cream print 1½" square to each short end of the two remaining units from step 3. Press the seam allowances toward the cream print square.

6. Sew the units made in step 5 to the remaining sides of the nine-patch unit. Press the seam allowances toward the block center.

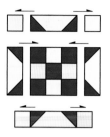 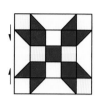

7. Repeat steps 1 through 6 to make 61 Farmer's Daughter blocks measuring 5½" square.

PIECING THE ROWS

1. Lay out 13 Snowball Variation blocks to make a row A. Join the blocks. Press the seam allowances all in one direction. Repeat to make a total of two A rows.

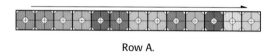

Row A.
Make 2.

2. Lay out seven Snowball Variation blocks and six Farmer's Daughter blocks in alternating positions to make a B row. Join the blocks. Press the seam allowances toward the Snowball Variation blocks. Repeat to make a total of six B rows.

Row B.
Make 6.

3. Lay out eight Snowball Variation blocks and five Farmer's Daughter blocks as shown to make a C row. Join the blocks. Press the seam allowances of the first and last Snowball Variation block toward the center of the row. Press the remaining seam allowances toward the Snowball Variation blocks. Repeat to make five C rows.

Row C.
Make 5.

ASSEMBLING THE QUILT TOP

1. Lay out six of row B and five of row C, alternating positions. Sew the rows together. Press the seam allowances open.

2. Join a row A to the top and bottom of the quilt top. Press the seam allowances toward the A rows. The pieced quilt top should now measure 65½" square.

COMPLETING THE QUILT

Refer to "Finishing Techniques" on page 18 for details as needed. Layer the quilt top, batting, and backing. Quilt the layers. The featured quilt was quilted in an overall swirling pattern. A pattern and guidelines for duplicating this design are provided in "Machine Quilting" on page 20. Join the 2½"-wide, random-length strips into one length and use it to bind the quilt.

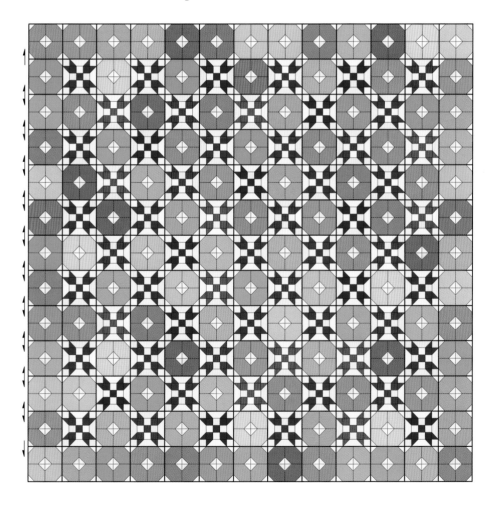

FEATHERED STARS

Gracefully arching plumes and richly hued stars blend our quilting heritage with a taste of modern style, and the result is simply spectacular. These aren't your grandmother's feathered stars!

SAW

Finished quilt: 52½" x 52½"
Block size: 12" x 12"

MATERIALS FOR WALL QUILT

Yardages are based on 42"-wide fabric. For greater ease of fabric selection and cutting, the yardage guidelines are provided separately for the patchwork and appliqué portions of this project.

PATCHWORK

- 28 fat eighths (or equivalent scraps) of assorted prints for star blocks and border
- 1⅝ yards of light tan print for patchwork and appliqué block backgrounds
- 1⅓ yards of black print for border and binding
- ⅞ yard of red print for border
- ⅜ yard of medium tan print for Star block backgrounds

APPLIQUÉ

- ⅜ yard of dark blue print for feathers
- 1 fat quarter of medium green plaid for stems
- 1 fat quarter of gold print for feathers
- 1 fat quarter of black print for flowers and flower centers
- 1 fat eighth of dark red plaid or print for berries

- 1 fat eighth of red stripe for flowers
- 1 fat eighth of gold print for flowers
- 1 fat eighth of medium green print for leaves
- 1 fat eighth of red print for flowers

OTHER

- 3⅜ yards of fabric for backing
- 59" x 59" piece of batting
- ⅜" bias bar

CUTTING

All strips are cut across the width of fabric unless otherwise noted. Refer to pages 102–103 for the appliqué patterns and to "Machine Appliqué" on page 24 for pattern piece preparation.

From the light tan print, cut:
- 8 strips, 1½" x 42"; crosscut into 96 rectangles, 1½" x 2½", and 32 squares, 1½" x 1½"
- 2 strips, 2½" x 42"; crosscut into 16 rectangles, 2½" x 4½"
- 2 strips, 4½" x 42"; crosscut into 16 squares, 4½" x 4½"
- 2 strips, 12½" x 42"; crosscut into 5 squares, 12½" x 12½"

From the medium tan print, cut:
- 3 strips, 1½" x 42"; crosscut into 64 squares, 1½" x 1½"
- 1 strip, 2½" x 42"; crosscut into 16 squares, 2½" x 2½"

(continued on page 95)

FEATHERED STARS WALL QUILT

Designed, machine pieced, and machine appliquéd by Kim Diehl. Machine quilted by Celeste Freiberg with hand-quilted accents by Kim Diehl.

From *each* of 24 assorted print fat eighths designated for the small Star blocks, cut:
- 1 square, 2½" x 2½" (total of 24)
- 8 squares, 1½" x 1½" (total of 192)

From *each* of the remaining 4 assorted print fat eighths designated for the large Star blocks, cut:
- 8 squares, 2½" x 2½" (total of 32)

From the remaining scraps of the assorted fat eighths, cut:
- 72 squares, 1½" x 1½", in matching sets of 2
- 36 rectangles, 2½" x 4½"

From the red print, cut:
- 4 strips, 2½" x 36½"
- 2 strips, 2½" x 42"; crosscut into 32 squares, 2½" x 2½"
- 5 strips, 1½" x 42"; crosscut into 40 rectangles, 1½" x 2½", and 20 rectangles, 1½" x 4½"

From the black print, cut:
- 4 strips, 2½" x 36½"
- 3 strips, 2½" x 42"; crosscut into 40 squares, 2½" x 2½"
- 4 strips, 1½" x 42"; crosscut into 32 rectangles, 1½" x 2½", and 16 rectangles, 1½" x 4½"
- 6 strips, 2½" x 42" (binding)

From the appliqué fabrics, cut the pieces for the corner blocks as follows:
- 4 from gold print using pattern A
- 4 from dark blue print using pattern B
- 4 from dark blue print using pattern B reversed
- 4 from the red stripe using pattern C
- 4 from gold print using pattern D
- 4 from black print using pattern E
- 20 from dark red plaid or print using pattern E
- 4 from medium green print using pattern F
- 4 from medium green print using pattern F reversed

- 8 from red print using pattern G
- 8 from black print using pattern H
- 8 from black print using pattern I
- 8 bias strips, 1¼" x 6½", from medium green plaid

From the appliqué fabrics, cut the pieces for the center block as follows:
- 4 from dark blue print using modified pattern B
- 4 from dark blue print using modified pattern B reversed
- 1 from red stripe using pattern C
- 1 from gold print using pattern D
- 1 from black print using pattern E
- 12 from gold print using pattern E
- 4 from medium green print using pattern F
- 4 from medium green print using pattern F reversed
- 4 from dark red plaid or print using pattern J

Piecing the Star Blocks

1. Using a mechanical pencil, lightly draw a diagonal line on the wrong side of the 24 sets of eight assorted print 1½" squares.

2. Select a prepared set of 1½" squares. With right sides together, layer one square over the end of a light tan print 1½" x 2½" rectangle. Sew together exactly on the drawn line. Press and trim, referring to "Pressing Triangle Units" on page 15. Repeat to layer a matching print square on the opposite end of the rectangle to form a mirror-image star point. Sew, press, and trim. Make four pieced rectangles from each set of prints for a total of 96 star point units.

Make 96.

3. Lay out four star point units, one matching print 2½" square, two light tan print 1½" squares, and two medium tan print 1½" squares in three horizontal rows to form block A as shown. Join the pieces to make the rows. Press seam allowances in the direction of the arrows. Join the rows. Press the seam allowances away from the star center. Repeat to make 16 of block A measuring 4½" square.

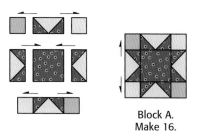

Block A.
Make 16.

4. Lay out four star point units, one matching print 2½" square, and four medium tan print 1½" squares in three horizontal rows to form block B. Sew and press as instructed in step 3. Make eight of block B measuring 4½" square.

Block B.
Make 8.

5. Lay out four of block A, one of block B, and four light tan print 4½" squares in three horizontal rows as shown. Join the pieces in each row. Press the seam allowances toward the tan print squares. Join the rows. Press the seam allowances toward the center row. Repeat to make four Star blocks measuring 12½" square. Reserve the four remaining B blocks for use in the border.

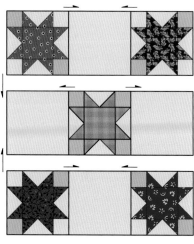

Make 4.

Appliquéing the Corner Blocks

1. Referring to "Preparing Background Fabric" on page 27, press a diagonal crease in each light tan print 12½" block. To preserve the seam allowances during the appliqué process, I recommend that you apply a thin line of Fray Check around the edges of the squares. Set aside one block for the quilt center.

2. Referring to "Machine Appliqué" on page 24, prepare the appliqués cut for the corner blocks.

3. Referring to "Making Bias-Tube Stems and Vines" on page 27, prepare the stems.

4. Center a prepared C flower appliqué over the crease on one corner of a prepared block, positioning it about 1" in from the raw edges on each side of the point. Pin or baste in place.

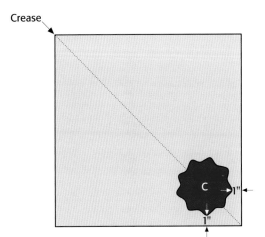

5. Using the C appliqué for placement, position the prepared A, B, and B reversed appliqués and the stems onto the block. Ensure that the raw edges are tucked under the C appliqué approximately ¼". Pin or baste the appliqués in place and remove the C appliqué. Referring to "Invisible Machine Appliqué" on page 28, stitch the appliqués to the block and then remove the paper pattern pieces.

6. Continue positioning and stitching the remaining appliqués, referring to the placement guide above right and working from the bottom layer to the top in alphabetical order. Remember to remove the paper from each appliqué before adding the next layer.

7. Repeat steps 4 through 6 for a total of four appliquéd corner blocks.

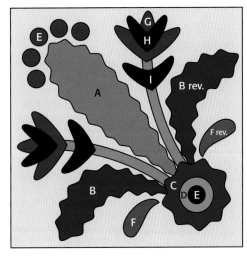

Make 4.

APPLIQUÉING THE CENTER BLOCK

1. Prepare the appliqués cut for the center block as you did for the corner blocks.

2. Using the reserved 12½" background block, press a second diagonal crease into the cloth. Center a prepared C appliqué over the intersecting creases and pin in place. Position the modified B and B reversed appliqués around the flower, tucking the raw edges under it approximately ¼". Pin or baste the appliqués in place. Remove the C appliqué and stitch the feathers to the block before removing the paper pattern pieces.

PERFECTLY CENTERED APPLIQUÉS

When a pattern instructs you to center a prepared appliqué over a pressed crease on a block background, try this trick. Carefully fold the appliqué in half and finger-press the midpoint crease at each prepared edge. Align the crease of the appliqué with the crease on the block and you'll achieve perfectly balanced results every time!

NEW LIFE FOR OLD MATS

Don't throw out your worn cutting mat! Turn it over and use the reverse side for a nonslip surface when tracing appliqué patterns or drawing stitching lines on patchwork pieces.

3. Continue positioning and stitching the remaining appliqués C, D, and E, working from the bottom layer to the top in alphabetical order. Remember to remove the paper pattern pieces from each appliqué before adding each new layer. Reserve the prepared F, F reversed, and J appliqués; they will be stitched later.

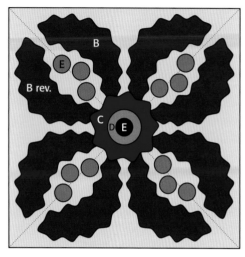

Make 1.

ASSEMBLING THE QUILT CENTER

1. Referring to the quilt diagram, lay out four Star blocks, four appliquéd corner blocks, and the appliquéd center block in three rows. Join the pieces in each horizontal row. Press the seam allowances toward the appliqué blocks, taking care

not to apply heat to the appliqués. Join the rows. Press the seam allowances away from the center row, again taking care when pressing the seams near the appliqués.

2. Stitch the reserved appliqués to the quilt center as shown. The finished quilt center should now measure 36½" square.

Piecing the Border Units

1. Using a mechanical pencil, lightly draw a diagonal line on the wrong side of the 72 assorted fat eighth 1½" squares, 32 red print 2½" squares, and 40 black print 2½" squares.

2. Select 20 matching pairs of marked assorted 1½" squares. With right sides together, layer a prepared 1½" square over one end of a red print 1½" x 2½" rectangle. Stitch, press, and trim. Repeat to make 20 pieced rectangles that are the mirror image of the first 20 as shown.

Make 20.

Make 20.

3. Sew two matching pieced rectangles from step 2 together as shown to form a small sawtooth unit. Press the seam allowance to one side. Sew a red print 1½" x 4½" rectangle to the top of the unit. Press the seam allowance toward the top rectangle. Repeat for a total of 20 small red sawtooth units.

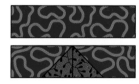

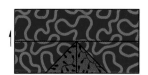

Make 20.

4. Repeat steps 2 and 3 using the remaining sets of prepared 1½" assorted squares, the black print 1½" x 2½" rectangles, and the black print 1½" x 4½" rectangles for a total of 16 small black sawtooth units.

Make 16. Make 16.

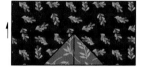

Make 16.

5. Layer a prepared red print 2½" square over one end of an assorted print 2½" x 4½" rectangle. Stitch, press, and trim. In the same manner, position a prepared red print 2½" square over the remaining end of the pieced rectangle in a mirror image. Stitch, press, and trim. Repeat to make 16 large, red flying-geese units.

6. Repeat step 5, using the 20 remaining assorted print 2½" x 4½" rectangles and 40 prepared 2½" black print squares, for a total of 20 large, black flying-geese units.

Assembling the Borders

1. Lay out five small, red flying-geese units and four large, red flying-geese units in alternating positions to form a sawtooth row. Join the units. Press the seam

allowances toward the large flying-geese units. Join a red print 2½" x 36½" strip to the point side of the sawtooth row. Press the seam allowance toward the red strip. Repeat for a total of four red sawtooth-border units.

Make 4.

2. Lay out four small, black flying-geese units and five large, black flying-geese units in alternating positions to form a sawtooth row. Join the units. Press the seam allowances toward the large flying-geese units. Join a black print 2½" x 36½" strip to the point side of the sawtooth row. Press the seam allowance toward the black strip. Repeat to make four black sawtooth-border units.

Make 4.

3. Join a red border unit and a black border unit along the pieced edges to complete a pieced border strip. Press the seam allowance toward the red. Repeat to make four pieced borders.

Make 4.

PIECING THE BORDER STAR BLOCKS

1. Using a mechanical pencil, lightly draw a diagonal line on the wrong side of the four sets of eight assorted print 2½" squares.

2. Make four matching sets of star point units using the assorted print 2½" fat eighth squares and the light tan print 2½" x 4½" rectangles.

Make 4 sets of 4 each.

3. Lay out four matching star point units, one reserved B block, and four medium tan 2½" squares in three horizontal rows to form a Star-in-a-Star block. Join the pieces in each row. Press the seam allowances of the top and bottom rows toward the inner star points. Press the seam allowances of the middle row away from the center star. Join the rows. Press the seam allowances away from the block center. Repeat to make four Star-in-a-Star blocks measuring 8½" square.

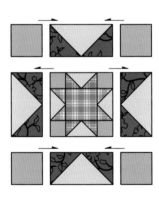

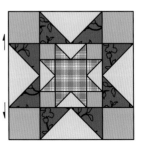

Make 4.

Adding the Borders

1. Join the red side of a sawtooth border unit to the right and left sides of the quilt center. Press the seam allowances toward the red print.

2. Sew a Star-in-a-Star block to each end of the remaining sawtooth border units. Press the seam allowances away from the Star-in-a-Star blocks. Join the pieced border units to the top and bottom of the quilt. Press the seam allowances toward the red print. The finished quilt top should measure 52½" square.

Completing the Quilt

Refer to "Finishing Techniques" on page 18 for details as needed. Layer the quilt top, batting, and backing. Quilt the layers. The background areas of the featured quilt were machine quilted in an overall pattern of free-form lines and shapes, with a stylized feathered cable stitched in the red portion of the borders. The stars, appliqué shapes, and sawtooth border triangles were hand quilted. Join the six black print 2½" x 42" strips into one length and use it to bind the quilt.

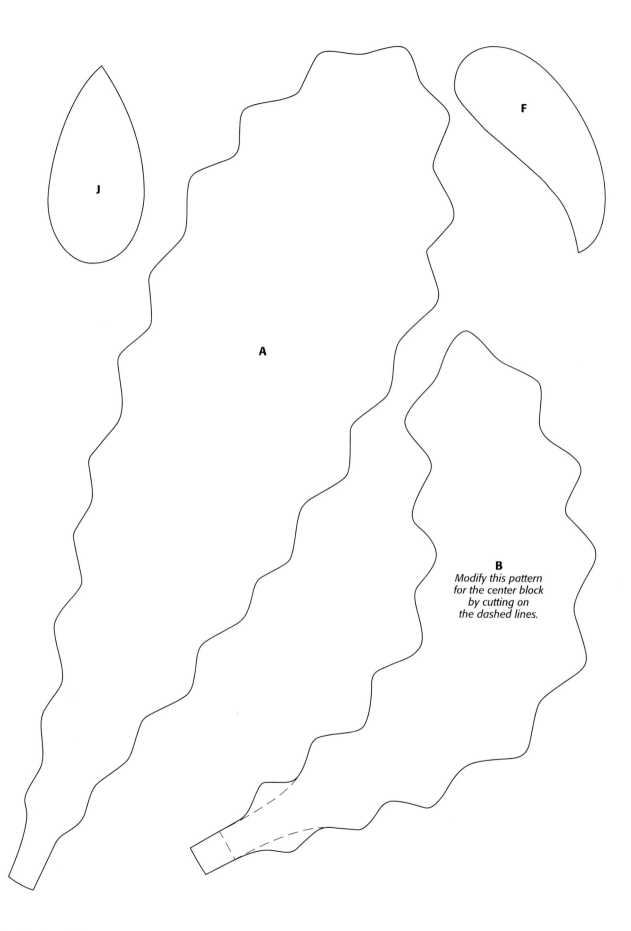

B
*Modify this pattern
for the center block
by cutting on
the dashed lines.*

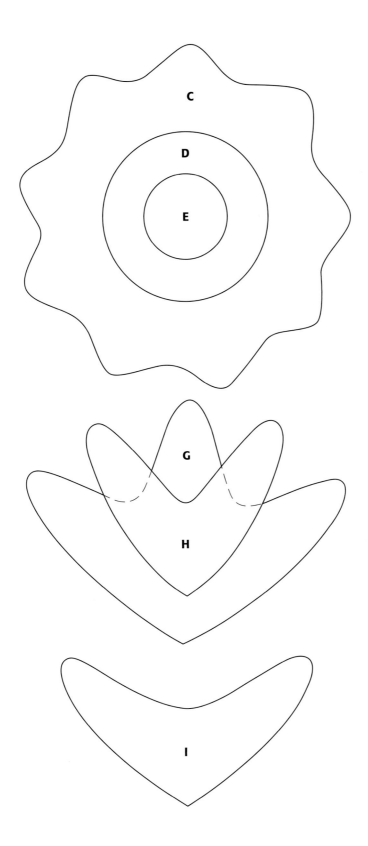

C

D

E

G

H

I

Garden Patch

Mischievous Nine Patch blocks seem to hopscotch through the garden, imploring you to catch them if you can. Indulge yourself and renew your spirit with this garden party that never ends.

Finished quilt: 65½" x 74½"
Finished blocks: 9" x 9"

Materials for Lap Quilt

Yardages are based on 42"-wide fabric.

- 2 yards of cream print for blocks and border
- 1¾ yards of medium blue plaid for border
- 1½ yards of dark blue print for appliqués and binding
- ⅞ yard of red print for appliqués
- ⅜ yard of dark green print for appliqués
- ⅓ yard of gold print for appliqués
- 1 strip *each*, 1½" x 42", of 25 assorted prints for blocks and border
- 2¼ yards *total* of homespun scraps or ¼ yard *each* of at least 9 different homespuns
- 4 yards of fabric for backing
- 72" x 81" piece of batting
- ⅜" bias bar

Cutting

All strips are cut across the width of fabric unless otherwise noted. Refer to page 111 for the appliqué patterns and to "Machine Appliqué" on page 24 for pattern piece preparation.

From *each* assorted print 1½" x 42" strip, cut:
- 2 strips, 1½" x 12", and 1 strip, 1½" x 6"

From the remaining scraps of assorted print 1½" x 42" strips, cut:
- 101 squares, 1½" x 1½"

From the cream print, cut:
- 22 strips, 1½" x 42"; crosscut into:
  - 25 strips, 1½" x 12"
  - 50 strips, 1½" x 6"
  - 101 squares, 1½" x 1½"
- 6 strips, 3½" x 42"; crosscut into 60 squares, 3½" x 3½"
- 1 strip, 9½" x 42"; crosscut into 4 squares, 9½" x 9½"

From the homespun scraps, cut:
- 75 squares, 3½" x 3½"
- 60 bias-cut squares, 3½" x 3½"

From the red print, cut:
- 4 strips, 1½" x 42"
- 24 using pattern C
- 96 using pattern G
- 4 using pattern B

(continued on page 107)

GARDEN PATCH LAP QUILT

Designed, machine pieced, and machine appliquéd by Kim Diehl.
Machine quilted by Celeste Freiberg.

From the gold print, cut:
- 4 strips, 1½" x 42"
- 28 using pattern D

From the dark blue print, cut:
- 8 strips, 2½" x 42" (binding)
- 12 strips, 1½" x 42"; crosscut into:
  - 8 strips, 1½" x 14"
  - 8 strips, 1½" x 10½"
  - 8 strips, 1½" x 8½"
  - 8 strips, 1½" x 4"
  - 28 strips, 1½" x 3"
- 32 using pattern E

From the dark green print, cut:
- 64 using pattern F

From the medium blue plaid, cut:
- 2 strips, 9½" x 56½", from the lengthwise grain
- 2 strips, 9½" x 47½", from the lengthwise grain

PIECING THE NINE PATCH BLOCKS

1. Sew a matching assorted print 1½" x 12" strip to each long side of a cream print 1½" x 12" strip. Press the seam allowances toward the darker print. Cut the strip set into six A segments measuring 1½" x 3½".

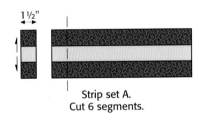

Strip set A.
Cut 6 segments.

2. Sew a cream print 1½" x 6" strip to each long side of an assorted print 1½" x 6" strip that matches the strips used in step 1. Press the seam allowances toward the darker print. Cut the strip set into three B segments measuring 1½" x 3½".

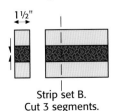

Strip set B.
Cut 3 segments.

3. Lay out two A segments and one B segment to form a nine-patch unit. Sew the rows together. Press the seam allowances away from the center row. Repeat to make three nine-patch units.

Make 3.

4. Repeat steps 1 through 3 with the remaining assorted print and cream 1½"-wide strips to make a total of 75 nine-patch units.

5. Lay out five nine-patch units with four cream print 3½" squares to form a block. Join the pieces in each horizontal row. Press the seam allowances toward the cream print squares. Sew the rows together. Press the seam allowances toward the center row. Repeat to make a total of 15 Nine Patch blocks measuring 9½" square.

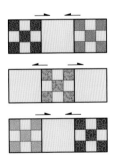 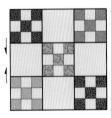

Make 15.

PIECING THE HOMESPUN BLOCKS

Lay out five homespun 3½" squares and four bias-cut homespun 3½" squares to form a nine-patch unit. Join the pieces in each horizontal row. Press the seam allowances toward the straight-grain blocks. Join the rows. Press the seam

STABILIZE BIAS-CUT PATCHWORK

When working with pieces that have bias edges, you may wish to take a moment to carefully stay-stitch them just inside the raw edges. This will help stabilize these delicate pieces and there will be less chance of stretching as you handle them.

allowances away from the center row. Repeat for a total of 15 Homespun blocks measuring 9½" square.

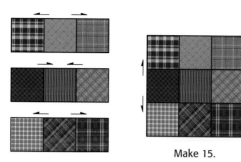

Make 15.

Assembling the Quilt Center

Lay out 15 Nine Patch blocks and 15 Homespun blocks in horizontal rows, alternating the placement of the blocks as shown in the quilt diagram. Sew the blocks together in each horizontal row. Press the seam allowances toward the Homespun blocks. Sew the rows together. Press the seam allowances in one direction. The pieced quilt center should measure 45½" x 54½".

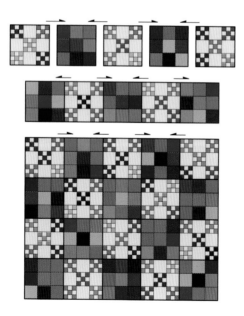

Piecing and Adding the Inner Border

1. Lay out 27 assorted print 1½" squares and 27 cream print 1½" squares in alternating positions to form a checkerboard strip. Join the squares. Press the seam allowances toward the assorted prints. Repeat for a total of two checkerboard strips. Join these strips to the right and left sides of the quilt center. Press the seam allowances toward the checkerboard strips.

2. Lay out 23 cream print 1½" squares and 24 assorted print 1½" squares, and sew them together as in step 1 to make the top border. Repeat with 24 cream print squares and 23 assorted print squares to make the bottom border. Sew these strips to the top and bottom of the quilt center. Press the seam allowances toward the checkerboard strips.

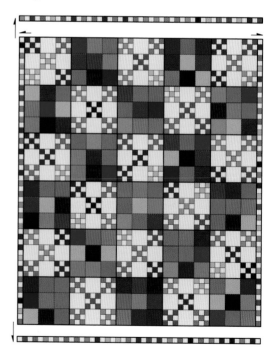

Appliquéing the Border Corner Blocks

1. Lay out four red print 1½" x 42" strips with four gold print 1½" x 42" strips, alternating their placement. Join the strips to form a strip set. Press the seam allowances toward the red print. Cut the strip set into 24 segments measuring 1½" x 8½".

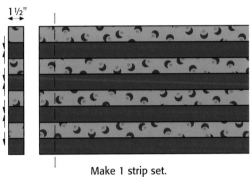

Make 1 strip set.
Cut 24 segments.

2. Lay out six checkerboard segments from step 1, reversing the direction of every other strip to form a checkerboard unit. Join the rows. Press the seam allowances in one direction. Repeat for a total of four checkerboard units measuring 6½" x 8½".

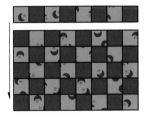

Make 4.

3. From each checkerboard unit, cut one appliqué using pattern A, for a total of four. Referring to "Machine Appliqué" on page 24, prepare the appliqués for stitching.

NOTE: I recommend adding a generous ¼" seam allowance to the A appliqués to make pressing the pieced seam allowances easier.

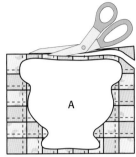

4. Prepare the remaining appliqués for stitching.

5. Referring to "Making Bias-Tube Stems and Vines" on page 27, prepare the dark blue stems using all of the various lengths of dark blue 1½"-wide strips.

6. Press a diagonal crease in each cream print 9½" square as instructed in "Preparing Background Fabric" on page 27.

7. Referring to the illustration, lay out the following: one A appliqué, one B appliqué, two F appliqués, one D appliqué, and one prepared 3" stem.

8. Remove all but the bottom appliqués, and pin or baste them in place. Referring to "Invisible Machine Appliqué" on page 28, stitch the pieces to the background. Work from the bottom layer to the top and remember to remove the paper pattern pieces before adding each new layer. Leave a small area un-stitched on each top side of the vase appliqué for adding the vines.

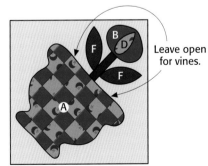

Leave open for vines.

ADDING THE OUTER BORDER

1. Sew a medium blue plaid 9½" x 56½" strip to the right and left sides of the quilt center. Press the seam allowances toward the blue plaid.

2. Sew an appliquéd 9½" border corner block to each end of the medium blue plaid 9½" x 47½" strips. Carefully press the seam allowances toward the medium blue plaid, taking care not to apply heat to the appliqués. Join these pieced strips to the top and bottom of the quilt. Press the seam allowances toward the blue plaid. The pieced quilt center should measure 65½" x 74½".

APPLIQUÉING THE OUTER BORDER

1. Lay out two prepared 14" vines in mirror-image positions over one border corner, tucking the ends into the openings at the top edge of the vase. To each 14" vine, add one side stem measuring 4" in length, one prepared 10½" stem, one prepared 8½" stem, and three prepared 3" stems. Ensure that all raw ends are tucked

under the vines where they meet, and then stitch them in place. Stitch the openings at the top of the vase. Repeat with each remaining corner of the quilt top.

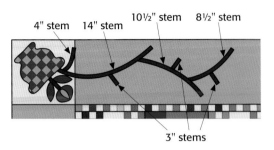

4" stem   14" stem   10½" stem   8½" stem

3" stems

2. Referring to the quilt photo on page 106 for placement, lay out the remaining appliqués along the vines and stems. Pin or baste the pieces in place, and work from the bottom layer to the top to stitch them to the borders. Remember to remove the paper pattern pieces before adding each new layer.

COMPLETING THE QUILT

Refer to "Finishing Techniques" on page 18 for details as needed. The featured quilt was machine quilted with a crosshatch design in the Nine Patch blocks and vases, and Xs were stitched in the checkerboard border. The Homespun blocks feature square feathered wreaths. Quilted accents were added to the leaf appliqués, with a feathered X design placed onto the open border areas. The remaining background portions of the quilt were filled in with a small stipple. Join the eight 2½" x 42" dark blue print strips into one length and use it to bind the quilt.

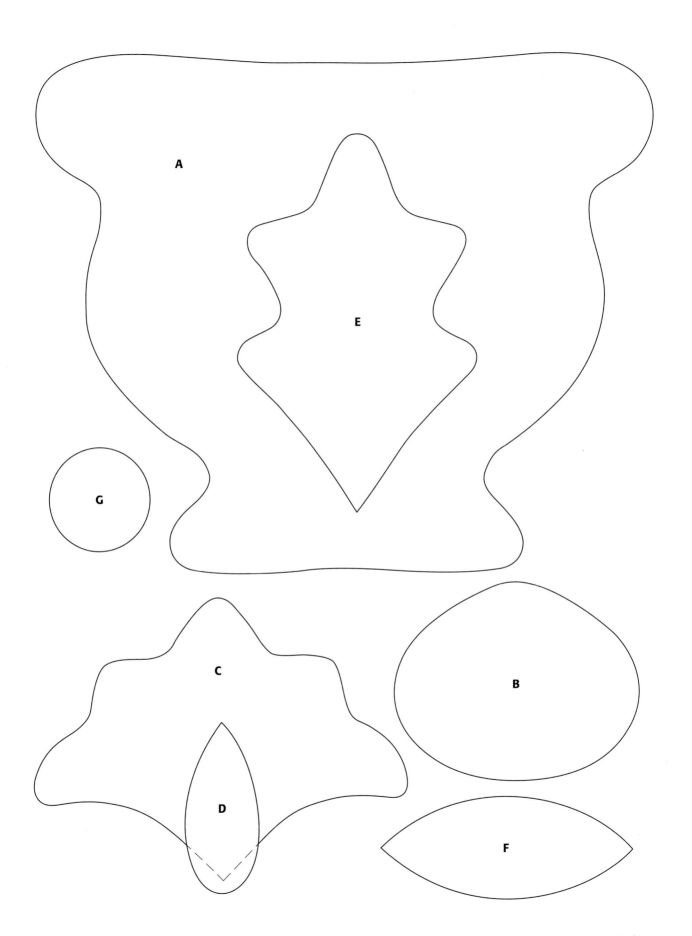

A

E

G

C

D

B

F

HARVEST HEART

Nature's bounty will forever flourish on the vine in this sweet and charming wall hanging with fanciful flowers. Tuck it into the tiniest niche or corner and treat yourself to a little touch of whimsy.

Finished quilt: 16½" x 22½"

MATERIALS FOR WALL QUILT

Yardages are based on 42"-wide fabric.

- ½ yard of brown print for border and binding
- 1 fat quarter of light neutral print for background
- 1 strip, 2½" x 42", of green stripe for stems and blocks
- 1 square, 7" x 7", of red print for heart
- Scraps of assorted prints for appliqués and border blocks
- ¾ yard of fabric for backing
- 23" x 29" piece of batting
- ⅜" bias bar

CUTTING

All strips are cut across the width of the fabric unless otherwise noted. Refer to page 117 for the appliqué patterns and to "Machine Appliqué" on page 24 for pattern piece preparation.

From the fat quarter of light neutral print, cut:
- 1 rectangle, 10½" x 16½"

From the 2½" x 42" strip of green stripe, cut:
- 1 strip, 1¼" x 10"
- 2 strips, 1¼" x 7"
- 1 strip, 1¼" x 9"
- 1 square, 2" x 2"

From the assorted print scraps, cut:
- 15 squares, 2" x 2"
- 1 *each* using patterns A, E, and E reversed
- 2 *each* using patterns B, C, D, F, and G
- 3 using pattern H
- 9 using pattern I

From the brown print, cut:
- 2 rectangles, 3½" x 16½"
- 2 rectangles, 3½" x 10½"
- 3 strips, 2½" x 42" (binding)

APPLIQUÉING THE CENTER BLOCK

1. Referring to "Preparing Background Fabric" on page 27, press a center vertical crease into the 10½" x 16½" piece of light neutral print.

2. Referring to "Making Bias-Tube Stems and Vines" on page 27, prepare the stems using the 1¼"-wide strips cut from the green stripe.

HARVEST HEART WALL QUILT

Designed, machine pieced, machine appliquéd, and hand quilted in the big-stitch method by Kim Diehl.

3. Set aside the 10" stem for later use. Fold each remaining stem in half with the seam allowances together, and use a pair of scissors to cut off the folded tip at a 45° angle. Each cut will yield two new stems with an angled tip. You should have a total of six stems. Keep these stems grouped in three pairs.

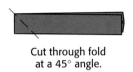

Cut through fold
at a 45° angle.

4. Lay out the three pairs of short stems cut in step 3 along the center crease as shown, positioning them at a 45° angle, with the longest pair placed in the middle. Pin or baste the stems in place. Lay the 10" stem over the pressed center line, positioning it approximately 2" down from the top raw edge and ensuring it covers the raw ends of the short stems. Pin or baste in place. Referring to "Invisible Machine Appliqué" on page 28, stitch the stems to the background.

NOTE: I recommend using liquid basting glue to attach the stems for stitching, because it will ensure that the stems remain securely anchored without any shifting of the side pieces.

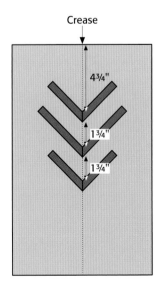

5. Referring to "Machine Appliqué" on page 24, prepare appliqué pieces A through I.

6. Position the prepared appliqués on the block background to ensure everything fits and is to your liking. When you are satisfied with their placement, remove all but the bottom-most appliqués and pin or baste them in place. Stitch the appliqués to the background and remove the paper pattern pieces.

7. Continue adding and stitching the remaining appliqués, working from the bottom layer to the top and remembering to remove the paper pattern pieces before adding each new layer.

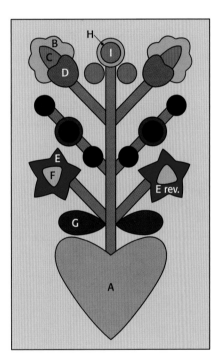

Piecing the Borders

1. Sew a brown print 3½" x 16½" rectangle to the right and left sides of the quilt center; press the seam allowances toward the brown print.

2. Join two assorted print 2" squares. Press the seam allowance to one side. Repeat with the remaining 2" squares for a total of eight joined pairs.

3. Join two pairs from step 2 to form a Four Patch block. Press the seam allowance to one side. Repeat to make 4 Four Patch blocks.

4. Sew a Four Patch block to each opposite end of the two brown print 3½" x 10½" rectangles. Press the seam allowances toward the brown print.

5. Sew a pieced border strip from step 4 to the top and bottom edges of the quilt center. Press the seam allowances toward the brown print. The finished quilt top should measure 16½" x 22½".

Completing the Quilt

Refer to "Finishing Techniques" on page 18 for details as needed. Layer the quilt top, batting, and backing. Quilt the layers. The featured quilt was hand quilted in the big-stitch method, with a 1" grid stitched behind the appliqués and the appliqués themselves outlined for emphasis. A row of feathers was stitched in the borders, with every other feather omitted for interest. The Four Patch blocks were quilted with an X pattern. Join the brown print 2½" x 42" strips into one length and use it to bind the quilt.

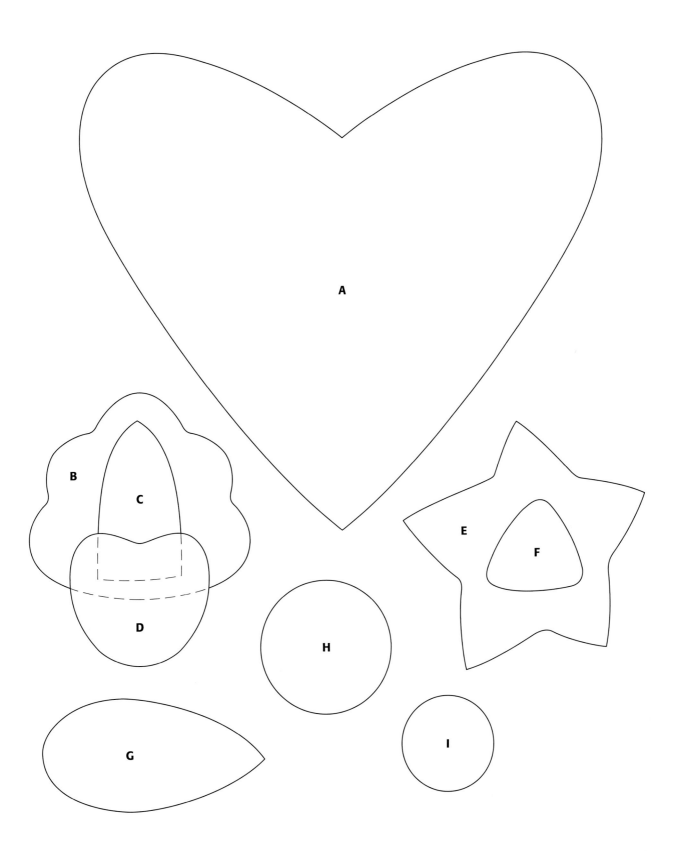

PRAIRIE PRIMROSE

Dream sweet dreams with this prairie of glorious appliqué vines as they burst forth into full bloom. Colorful ribbon fences with penny-style posts will entice you to cultivate a sun-dappled prairie of your own.

Finished quilt: 103½" x 103½"
Finished block: 20" x 20"

NOTE: Each block in the quilt center and border corners features two prints. To simplify your fabric selection and cutting, designate these two prints as fabric #1 and fabric #2 as you choose your assorted prints. Have fun with the fabric selection process, because it provides the perfect opportunity for you to experiment.

MATERIALS FOR BED QUILT

Yardages are based on 42"-wide fabric.

- 7 yards *total* of assorted prints for blocks, sashing, and border
- 4¼ yards of light neutral print for border
- 3½ yards of medium green print for stems, leaf appliqués, border, and binding
- 9 squares, 20½" x 20½", of light neutral prints for block backgrounds
- 3 yards *total* of assorted light neutral prints for corner posts and sashing
- Assorted green print scraps for leaf appliqués
- 9¼ yards of fabric for backing
- 110" x 110" piece of batting
- ⅜" bias bar

CUTTING

All strips are cut across the width of the fabric unless otherwise noted. Refer to pages 124–125 for the appliqué patterns and to "Machine Appliqué" on page 24 for pattern piece preparation.

From the medium green print, cut:
- 11 strips, 2" x 42"
- 11 strips, 2½" x 42" (binding)
- Enough 1¼"-wide bias lengths to make a 1,052" strip (29 yards and 8")
- 24 using pattern F

From the assorted prints, cut the following block appliqués:
- 9 using pattern A (1 from each fabric #1)
- 18 using pattern B (2 from each fabric #2)
- 9 using pattern C (1 from each fabric #1)
- 117 using pattern D (13 from each fabric #2)
- 108 using pattern E (12 from each fabric #1)

From the assorted prints, cut the following corner post appliqués:
- 16 using pattern C
- 16 using pattern D

From the assorted prints, cut the following border appliqués:
- 56 using pattern D
- 56 using pattern E

(continued on page 121)

Prairie Primrose Bed Quilt

Designed, machine pieced, and machine appliquéd by Kim Diehl.
Machine quilted by Celeste Freiberg.

From the assorted prints, cut the following border corner block appliqués:

- 4 using pattern A (1 from each fabric #1)
- 8 using pattern B (2 from each fabric #2)
- 4 using pattern C (1 from each fabric #1)
- 4 using pattern D (1 from each fabric #2)

From the remaining assorted prints, cut:

- 896 squares, 1¾" x 1¾", in matching sets of 4
- 224 squares, 3" x 3" (1 square to match each set cut above)

From the assorted green print scraps, cut:

- 104 using pattern F

From the assorted light neutral prints, cut:

- 448 rectangles, 1¾" x 3"
- 16 squares, 5½" x 5½"
- 4 squares, 10½" x 10½"

From the light neutral print for the border, cut:

- 4 strips, 10½" x 70½", from the lengthwise grain

Preparing the Stems

1. Stitch and press the medium green print 1,052" strip as instructed in "Making Bias-Tube Stems and Vines" on page 27.

2. Cut the prepared strip into the following lengths: 9 pieces measuring 60" long, 4 pieces measuring 72" long, and 56 pieces measuring 4" long.

Appliquéing the Center Blocks

The following instructions are written to make one block at a time.

1. Select one light neutral print 20½" block background and one 60" length of prepared vine. Cut the vine into four stems that are 7" long, four stems that are 4½" long, and four stems that are 3" long. Referring to "Preparing Background Fabric" on page 27, press vertical, horizontal, and diagonal creases in the background.

2. Select one matching set of appliqué pieces A, C, and E, and one matching set of appliqué pieces B and D. Choose eight assorted green print F appliqué pieces. Referring to "Machine Appliqué" on page 24, prepare the appliqué pieces.

3. Carefully fold the prepared A appliqué in half vertically, then horizontally, and finger-press a crease at the center position of each edge. Align these creases with the pressed creases in the background to center the appliqué on the block. Pin in place.

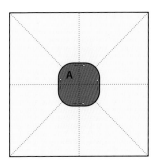

4. Lay out a prepared 7" stem with one raw end positioned under the A appliqué where it meets the diagonal crease. Next, add a 4½" stem, and then a 3" stem, tucking the raw ends under the first stem. Pin or baste in place. Repeat in each corner of the block.

NOTE: I dot the underside of each stem with liquid basting glue as I lay it out to eliminate the need for pinning or basting.

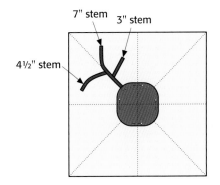

7" stem   3" stem   4½" stem

5. When you are satisfied with the stem positioning, remove the A appliqué and stitch the stems in place, referring to "Invisible Machine Appliqué" on page 28.

6. Next, lay out the A appliqué, and the D and F appliqués that are positioned along the stems. Pin or baste, and then stitch them in place. Continue adding and stitching the remaining appliqués, working from the bottom layer to the top and remembering to remove the paper pattern pieces before adding each new layer.

7. Repeat steps 1 through 6 to make nine appliquéd blocks.

Make 9.

APPLIQUÉING THE CORNER POSTS

1. Prepare the 16 C and D appliqué pieces.

2. Finger-press vertical and horizontal creases in each C and D appliqué. Press vertical and horizontal creases in the 16 assorted light neutral 5½" squares.

3. Use the pressed creases to center the appliqués on the background and work from the bottom layer to the top to stitch them in place. Repeat for a total of 16 appliquéd corner posts.

Make 16.

PIECING THE SASHING

1. Draw a diagonal line on the wrong side of the 896 assorted print 1¾" squares.

2. Select an assorted print 3" square, four matching prepared 1¾" squares, and two assorted light neutral print 1¾" x 3" rectangles. With right sides together, align a 1¾" square over one end of each neutral print rectangle. Sew the pair together exactly on the drawn line. Press and trim as instructed in "Pressing Triangle Units" on page 15.

Make 2.

3. In the same manner, layer a 1¾" square over the remaining end of each pieced rectangle, placing it in a mirror-image position. Sew, press, and trim as before to make two flying-geese units.

Make 2.

4. Join a flying-geese unit to two opposite sides of a matching print 3" square. Press the seam allowances toward the center square to make a sashing unit.

  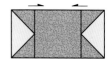

5. Repeat steps 2 through 4 to make a total of 224 sashing units.

6. Lay out eight sashing units to form a strip. Join the units. Press the seam allowances in one direction. Repeat to make a total of 24 sashing strips. Reserve the remaining sashing units for later use.

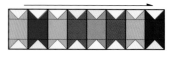

Make 24.

ASSEMBLING THE QUILT CENTER

1. Lay out four appliquéd corner posts and three sashing strips in alternating positions. Join the pieces end to end. Press the seam allowances toward the corner posts, taking care not to apply heat to the appliqués. Repeat to make four sashing rows.

Make 4.

2. Lay out four sashing strips and three appliquéd center blocks in alternating positions. Join the pieces. Press the seam allowances toward the appliquéd blocks, taking care when pressing near the appliqués. Repeat to make three block rows.

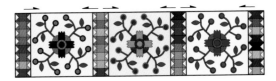

Make 3.

3. Referring to the quilt photo, lay out four sashing rows and three block rows to form the quilt center. Sew the rows together. Press the seam allowances toward the block rows, again taking care when applying heat near the appliqués. The quilt center should measure 80½" square.

MAKING THE APPLIQUÉD BORDER

1. Press a lengthwise center crease in each light neutral print 10½" x 70½" border strip.

2. Lay out a 72" prepared vine and 14 prepared 4" stems. Make sure that the vine is centered over the pressed crease with the ends of the 4" stems tucked under it, and pin or baste in place. Stitch the vine and stems to the foundation. Repeat to make four vine-embellished border strips.

3. Prepare the 56 D, E, and F appliqués for machine appliqué.

4. Lay out and stitch 14 prepared D, E, and F appliqués to each border strip, working from the bottom layer to the top. Remember to remove the paper pattern pieces before adding each new layer.

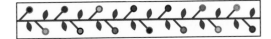

5. Press a vertical and horizontal crease in each assorted light neutral print 10½" square. Prepare the remaining A, B, C, and D appliqués.

6. Select a prepared A and C appliqué cut from one print, and two prepared B appliqués and a D appliqué cut from one print. Working from the bottom layer to the top, use creases to center and stitch the appliqués to the background. Repeat to make four appliquéd corner blocks.

Make 4.

7. Lay out four of the reserved sashing units and sew the pieces together. Press the seam allowances in one direction. Repeat to make a total of eight border sashing strips.

Make 8.

8. Sew a sashing strip to each short end of an appliquéd border strip using care near the appliqués. Press the seam allowances toward the sashing strips. Repeat to make four border strips.

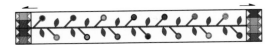

Make 4.

9. Sew a border strip from step 8 to the right and left sides of the quilt center. Press the seam allowances toward the border strips again, pressing with care near the appliqués.

10. Sew a 10½" appliquéd corner block to each short end of the remaining two border strips. Press the seam allowances toward the sashing strips. Sew these strips to the top and bottom of the quilt. Carefully press the seam allowances toward the border strips.

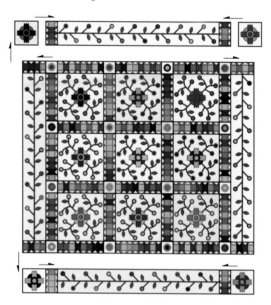

Adding the Outer Border

1. Sew 11 medium green print 2" x 42" strips together end to end. Press the seam allowances in one direction. Cut this strip into two lengths measuring 2" x 100½", and two lengths measuring 2" x 103½".

2. Sew a 2" x 100½" strip to the right and left sides of the quilt. Press the seam allowances toward the green strips. Sew a 2" x 103½" strip to the top and bottom of the quilt. Press the seam allowances toward the green strips. The quilt top should measure 103½" square.

Completing the Quilt

Refer to "Finishing Techniques" on page 18 for details as needed. Layer the quilt top, batting, and backing. Quilt the layers. The quilt featured was machine quilted with a medallion design stitched over the center of each appliquéd block. Leaves were quilted onto open background areas along the stems and vines to create a shadow effect, and a stipple design was stitched in the remaining background fabric. Feathered cables were stitched in the pieced sashing strips. Join the 11 medium green print 2½" x 42" strips into one length of binding and use it to bind the quilt.

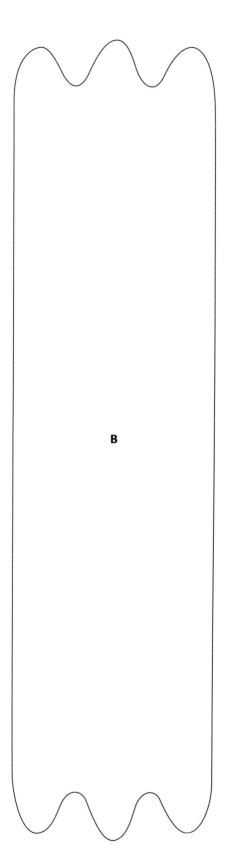

B

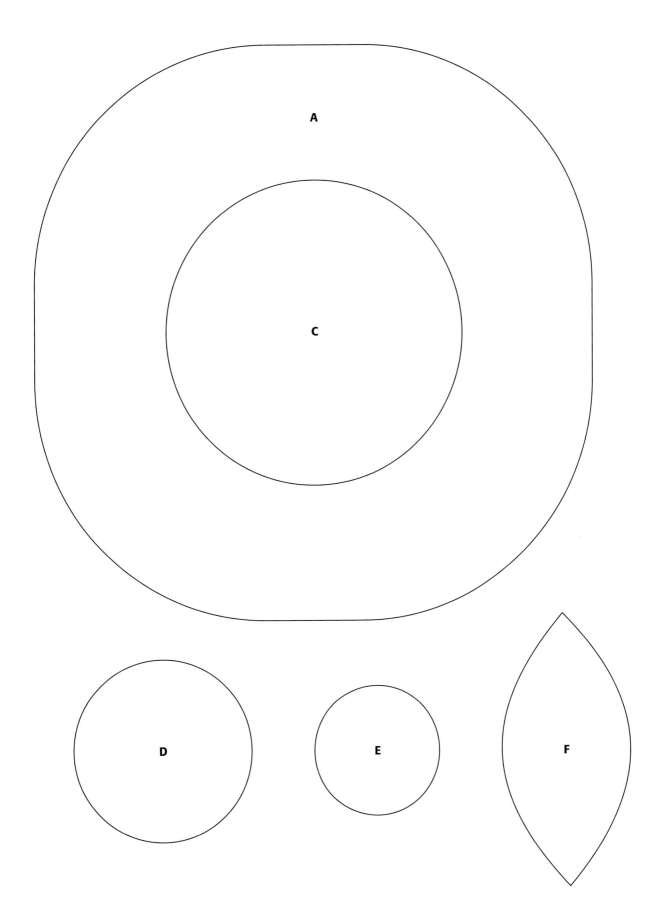

126

HUMBLE PIE

Star-spangled blossoms encircle strips of simple homespuns and muted prints for an effect that's anything but humble. You'll enjoy a slice of pure heaven when you nestle into this quilt's welcoming embrace.

Finished quilt: 64½" x 70½"
Finished blocks: 6" x 6"

MATERIALS FOR LAP QUILT
Yardages are based on 42"-wide fabric.

- ¼ yard *each* of 12 assorted homespuns and prints for blocks
- 2 yards of khaki homespun for outer border
- ⅞ yard of navy homespun for inner border #3 and binding
- 6 fat eighths (or scraps) of assorted dark green prints and homespuns for leaf appliqués
- ⅝ yard of blue print for Log Cabin border
- ½ yard of dark green homespun for Log Cabin border
- ½ yard of orange print for Log Cabin border
- ⅓ yard of gold print for Log Cabin border
- ¼ yard *each* of tan and brown homespuns for inner borders #1 and #2
- ¼ yard of gray homespun for Log Cabin border
- ¼ yard of dark green stripe for stems
- 1 strip, 1½" x 42", of cranberry print for Log Cabin border
- ¾ yard *total* of assorted print and plaid scraps for appliqués
- 4 yards of fabric for backing
- 71" x 77" piece of batting
- ⅜" bias bar

CUTTING
All strips are cut across the width of fabric unless otherwise noted. To simplify the process, cutting instructions are provided separately for each section of the quilt. Refer to page 133 for the appliqué pattern pieces and to "Machine Appliqué" on page 24 for pattern piece preparation.

CENTER BLOCKS
From *each* of the 12 assorted ¼-yard cuts of homespuns and prints, cut:
- 3 strips, 1½" x 42½"

INNER BORDERS
From the tan homespun, cut:
- 2 strips, 1½" x 36½"
- 2 strips, 1½" x 32½"

From the brown homespun, cut:
- 2 strips, 1½" x 38½"
- 2 strips, 1½" x 34½"

From the navy homespun, cut:
- 2 strips, 1½" x 40½"
- 2 strips, 1½" x 36½"

LOG CABIN BORDER BLOCKS
From the gray homespun, cut:
- 1 strip, 1½" x 42"
- 2 strips, 1½" x 42"; crosscut into 26 rectangles, 1½" x 2½"

(continued on page 129)

HUMBLE PIE LAP QUILT

Designed, machine pieced, machine appliquéd, and hand quilted in the big-stitch method by Kim Diehl.

From the gold print, cut:
- 5 strips, 1½" x 42"; crosscut into:
  - 26 rectangles, 1½" x 3½"
  - 26 rectangles, 1½" x 2½"
  - 4 squares, 1½" x 1½"

From the dark green homespun, cut:
- 8 strips, 1½" x 42½"; crosscut into:
  - 26 rectangles, 1½" x 4½"
  - 26 rectangles, 1½" x 3½"
  - 4 rectangles, 1½" x 3½"
  - 4 rectangles, 1½" x 2½"
  - 4 squares, 1½" x 1½"

From the orange print, cut:
- 9 strips, 1½" x 42"; crosscut into:
  - 30 rectangles, 1½" x 5½"
  - 30 rectangles, 1½" x 4½"
  - 4 rectangles, 1½" x 3½"
  - 4 rectangles, 1½" x 2½"

From the blue print, cut:
- 10 strips, 1½" x 42"; crosscut into:
  - 30 rectangles, 1½" x 6½"
  - 30 rectangles, 1½" x 5½"
  - 4 rectangles, 1½" x 4½"

Outer Border
From the khaki homespun, cut:
- 2 strips, 8½" x 54½", from the lengthwise grain
- 2 strips, 8½" x 64½", from the lengthwise grain

From the assorted prints and plaid scraps, cut:
- 14 *each* using patterns A and E, in matching prints
- 14 *each* using patterns B and F, in matching prints

From the fat eighths of assorted dark green prints and homespuns, cut:
- 84 using pattern C
- 14 using pattern D

From the dark green stripe, cut:
- 4 strips, 1½" x 42"

Binding
From the navy homespun, cut:
- 8 strips, 2½" x 42"

Assembling the Quilt Center

1. To make strip set A, select 6 different strips cut from the 12 assorted ¼-yard cuts. Sew the strips together along the long raw edges. Press the seam allowances in one direction. Repeat to make three of strip set A.

2. Cut the strip sets at 6½" intervals for a total of 15 A segments.

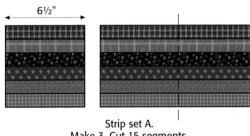

Strip set A.
Make 3. Cut 15 segments.

3. Repeat steps 1 and 2 using the remaining six fabrics to make 15 B segments.

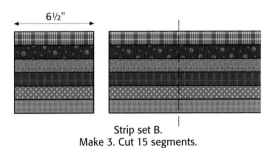

Strip set B.
Make 3. Cut 15 segments.

4. Referring to the quilt diagram on page 130, lay out the A and B segments in alternating positions to form six horizontal rows of five blocks each. Join the segments in each row. Press the seam allowances toward the segments with the vertical strips. Join the rows. Press the seam allowances in one direction. The pieced quilt center should measure 30½" x 36½".

BRUSHED COTTONS FOR VERSATILITY

Consider incorporating brushed cottons when a pattern calls for homespuns, because they can be very versatile for quiltmaking. The flat, smooth side is perfect for patchwork or appliqué, while the brushed side feels like flannel and makes a wonderful choice for a backing.

ADDING THE INNER BORDERS

1. Sew a tan 1½" x 36½" strip to the right and left sides of the quilt center. Press the seam allowances toward the tan strips. Sew a tan 1½" x 32½" strip to the top and bottom. Press the seam allowances toward the tan strips.

2. Sew a brown 1½" x 38½" strip to the right and left sides of the quilt. Press the seam allowances toward the brown strips. Sew a brown 1½" x 34½" strip to the top and bottom. Press the seam allowances toward the brown strips.

3. Sew a navy 1½" x 40½" strip to the right and left sides of the quilt top. Press the seam allowances toward the navy strips. Sew a navy 1½" x 36½" strip to the top and bottom. Press the seam allowances toward the navy strips.

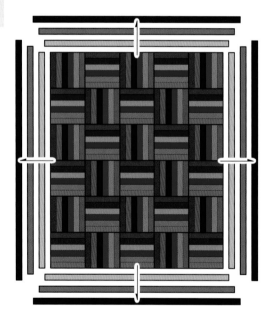

ASSEMBLING THE LOG CABIN BORDER

Using the pieces cut for the Log Cabin border blocks, refer to the block diagrams as you piece the blocks.

1. Join the cranberry and gray 1½" x 42" strips along the long edges to form a strip set. Press the seam allowances toward the cranberry print. Cut the strip set at 1½" intervals to make 26 segments.

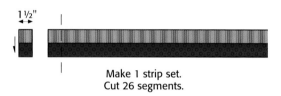

1½"

Make 1 strip set.
Cut 26 segments.

2. Sew a gray 1½" x 2½" rectangle to a segment from step 1. Press the seam allowance toward the gray rectangle. Continue adding rectangles in numerical order, pressing the seam allowance toward each new rectangle as it is added. Make 26 Log Cabin A blocks measuring 6½" square.

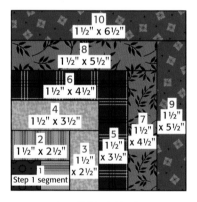

10
1½" x 6½"

8
1½" x 5½"

6
1½" x 4½"

4
1½" x 3½"

2
1½" x 2½"

3
1½" x 2½"

1
Step 1 segment

5
1½" x 4½"

7
1½" x 4½"

9
1½" x 5½"

Log Cabin A block.
Make 26.

3. Sew a gold 1½" square and a dark green 1½" square together. Press the seam allowance toward the dark green. Sew a dark green 1½" x 2½" rectangle to the first unit. Press the seam allowance toward the green rectangle. Continue adding rectangles in numerical order, pressing the seam allowance toward each new rectangle as it is added. Make four Log Cabin B blocks measuring 6½" square.

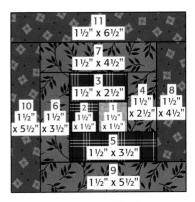

Log Cabin B block.
Make 4.

4. Join seven Log Cabin A blocks to form a side border strip. Press the seam allowances in one direction. Repeat for two border strips. Sew a border to each long side of the quilt top. Press the seam allowance toward the navy border.

Make 2.

5. Repeat step 4 using six Log Cabin A blocks to make two pieced top and bottom border strips. Sew a Log Cabin B block to each end of the pieced borders. Press the seam allowances toward the B blocks. Join these pieced strips to the remaining edges of the quilt top. Press the seam allowances toward the navy border.

Make 2.

ADDING THE OUTER BORDER

1. Referring to "Preparing Background Fabric" on page 27, press a lengthwise crease down the center of each khaki homespun border strip.

2. Join a prepared khaki 8½" x 54½" strip to the right and left sides of the quilt top. Press the seam allowances toward the khaki strips.

3. Join a prepared khaki 8½" x 64½" strip to the remaining edges of the quilt top. Press the seam allowances toward the khaki strips. The quilt top should measure 64½" x 70½".

APPLIQUÉING THE BORDERS

1. Referring to "Making Bias-Tube Stems and Vines" on page 27, prepare four dark green stripe 1½" x 42" strips for stems. Cut the prepared lengths into eight stems measuring 8½" long for the side borders, and six stems measuring 10½" long for the top and bottom borders.

2. Referring to "Machine Appliqué" on page 24, prepare the appliqué pieces.

3. Before beginning the appliqué process, I recommend that you apply a thin line of Fray Check around the perimeter of the quilt top to preserve the seam allowances and prevent fraying.

4. Arrange the stems and appliqués on the border strips, positioning them at even intervals around the perimeter of the quilt and using the pressed center creases for placement. Remove all but the bottommost pieces and pin or baste them in place. Referring to "Invisible Machine Appliqué"

on page 28, stitch the pieces in place, working from the bottom layer to the top and remembering to remove the paper pattern pieces before adding each new layer.

COMPLETING THE QUILT

Refer to "Finishing Techniques" on page 18 for details as needed. Layer the quilt top, batting, and backing. Quilt the layers together. The featured quilt was quilted with the big-stitch method and the block seams outlined ¼" from each sewn seam. A vertical and horizontal basket-weave design from the quilt center was stitched in the outer-border background, and the appliqués were outlined for emphasis. Join the navy homespun 2½" x 42" strips into one length and use it to bind the quilt.

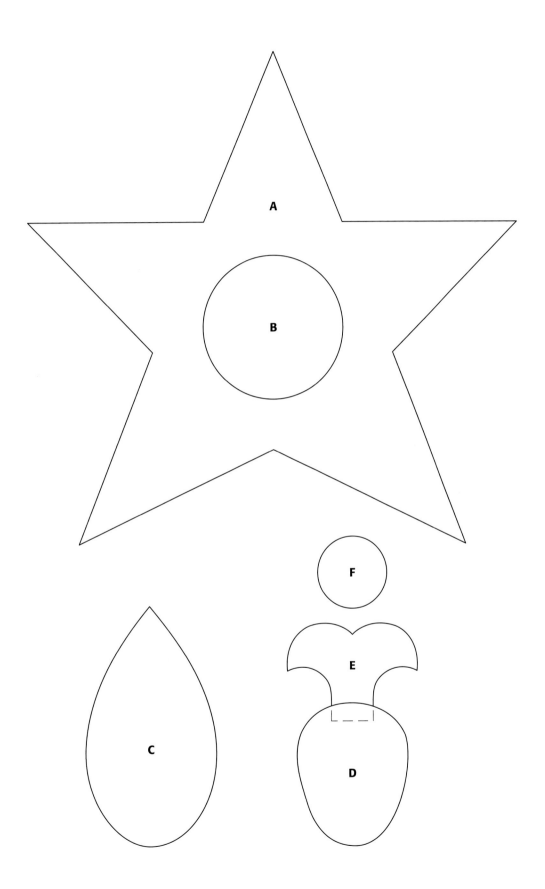

PASSING FANCY

Create an heirloom to be treasured when you fashion these striking blocks in dazzling hues. Adorn your quilt with meandering vines and a sprinkling of berries for an effect that's sure to take your fancy.

Finished quilt: 70½" x 70½"
Finished block: 5" x 5"

MATERIALS FOR LAP QUILT

Yardages are based on 42"-wide fabric.

- 5¼ yards of cream print for block and border backgrounds
- 3⅛ yards *total* of assorted dark prints for blocks, appliqués, and binding
- 2 yards *total* of assorted coordinating medium prints for blocks and appliqués
- 1 yard of green plaid for vines and leaf appliqués
- Scraps of assorted green prints for leaf appliqués
- 4⅓ yards of fabric for backing
- 77" x 77" piece of batting
- ⅜" bias bar
- Water-soluble marker
- Liquid basting glue

CUTTING

All strips are cut across the width of fabric unless otherwise noted. Refer to pages 142–143 for the appliqué pattern pieces and to "Machine Appliqué" on page 24 for pattern piece preparation. To make best use of your yardages, please cut the pieces in the order given. Note that each block features a medium and dark print of the same color.

From the cream print, cut:
- 4 strips, 10½" x 50½", from the lengthwise grain

From the remaining cream print, cut:
- 4 squares, 10½" x 10½"
- 400 squares, 1⅞" x 1⅞"; cut each square in half diagonally once to yield 800 triangles
- 200 squares, 2½" x 2½"
- 200 squares, 1½" x 1½"

From the assorted dark prints, cut:
- 400 squares, 1⅞" x 1⅞", in matching sets of 4. Cut each square in half diagonally once to yield 800 triangles.
- 100 squares, 1½" x 1½" (1 square to match each set of 4 squares cut above)
- Enough 2½"-wide lengths to make a 292" length of binding

From the assorted coordinating medium prints, cut:
- 200 rectangles, 1½" x 2½", in matching sets of 2
- 200 squares, 1½" x 1½" (in sets of 2 to match the rectangles cut above)

From the scraps of assorted medium *and* dark prints, cut:
- 52 using pattern A
- 52 using pattern B
- 152 using pattern D

(continued on page 137)

Passing Fancy Lap Quilt

Designed by Kim Diehl. Machine pieced by Penny Stephenson. Hand and machine appliquéd by Kim Diehl. Machine quilted by Celeste Freiberg.

From the green plaid, cut:

- Enough 1¼"-wide bias lengths to make a 535" length strip (14 yards and 31")

From scraps of the green plaid and assorted green prints, cut:

- 240 using pattern C (or a combination of C and C reversed)

NOTE: The featured quilt uses leaves prepared from pattern C and pattern C reversed placed randomly along the vines for added interest.

Piecing the Blocks

Since the blocks are scrappy, the instructions below are for sewing one block at a time. For one block you'll need the following:

- 8 cream print triangles
- 2 cream print squares, 2½" x 2½"
- 2 cream print squares, 1½" x 1½"
- 8 matching dark print triangles
- 1 matching dark print square, 1½" x 1½"
- 2 matching medium print rectangles, 1½" x 2½"
- 2 matching medium print squares, 1½" x 1½"

1. Align a dark print triangle with a cream print triangle. Sew the pair together along the long sides, taking care not to stretch the bias edges. Press the seam allowances toward the dark print. Trim away the dog-ear points. Repeat to make eight matching half-square-triangle units.

Make 8.

2. Join two half-square-triangle units. Press the seam allowances toward the cream print. Repeat to make two double-point units.

Make 2.

3. Sew a half-square-triangle unit to a cream print 1½" square. Press the seam allowances toward the cream print. Repeat for a total of two single-point units.

Make 2.

4. Sew a half-square-triangle unit to a medium print 1½" square. Press the seam allowances toward the medium print. Repeat for a total of two center units.

Make 2.

5. Sew a double-point unit from step 2 to a medium print 1½" x 2½" rectangle. Press the seam allowances toward the medium print. Repeat for a total of two pieced units.

Make 2.

If you wish to make a patchwork quilt without the appliqué embellishments that are featured in the border, simply make four extra blocks in a size to fit the border width, and position them in the corners. This will give your quilt a balanced look, and you'll never miss the appliqué!

6. Sew a cream print 2½" square and a single-point unit from step 2 to the unit made in step 5. Press the seam allowances away from the center unit. Repeat to make two row units.

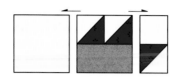

Make 2.

7. Sew a center unit from step 4 to opposite sides of a dark print 1½" square in mirror-image positions. Press the seam allowances toward the dark print.

8. Lay out the block segments in three rows as shown. Join the rows. Press the seam allowances away from the center row.

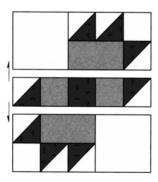

9. Repeat steps 1 through 8 to make a total of 100 blocks measuring 5½" square.

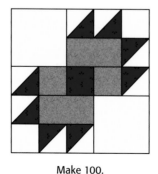

Make 100.

ASSEMBLING THE QUILT CENTER

1. Lay out 10 blocks to form row A, with every other block placed in a mirror-image position as shown. Join the blocks. Press the seam allowances to the right. Repeat to make five of row A.

Row A.
Make 5.

2. Lay out 10 blocks to form a mirror-image row B. Join the blocks. Press the seam allowances to the left. Repeat to make five of row B.

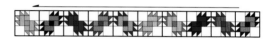

Row B.
Make 5.

3. Referring to the quilt diagram, lay out rows A and B in alternating positions. Join the rows. Press the seam allowances in one direction. The pieced quilt center should measure 50½" square.

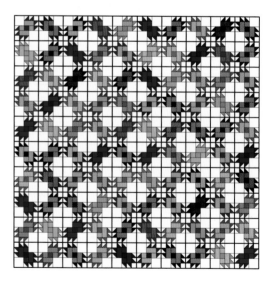

Appliquéing the Borders

1. Referring to "Machine Appliqué" on page 24, prepare the appliqué pieces.

2. Stitch and press the green plaid 535"-long bias strip as instructed in "Making Bias-Tube Stems and Vines" on page 27. From the prepared vine, cut 4 pieces, 65" long; 40 pieces, 4½" long; 4 pieces, 18" long; and 4 pieces, 3½" long.

3. Using two layers of freezer paper, make templates using the vine placement guide, stem placement guide, and wreath placement guide patterns on pages 142 and 143; include any dashed lines.

4. Before beginning the appliqué process, I recommend that you apply a thin line of Fray Check around the perimeter of each border strip to preserve the seam allowances. Press a vertical and horizontal center crease in each border strip as instructed in "Preparing Background Fabric" on page 27.

5. Lay a prepared cream print 10½" x 50½" border strip on a flat surface and smooth away any wrinkles. Position the vine placement guide on the border strip in the center where the creases meet. Align the straight edge along the horizontal crease. Use a water-soluble marker to trace the curve of the guide onto the cloth. Flip the guide over in a mirror-image position, with the end positioned where the first traced curve stops, and mark the next curve. Continue marking the vine curves in this manner, working from the center out to each end. Repeat to mark the four border strips.

6. Place tiny dots of liquid basting glue along the marked curves of one border strip, leaving a small area at the crest of each curve free of glue. Beginning at one end, press a prepared 65" length of vine down onto the line of glue, easing it around the curves. Trim away any excess vine length. Repeat to make four vine-embellished borders.

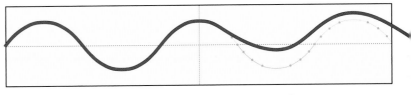

Make 4.

7. Lay out a border strip from step 6. Use the vine placement guide and a water-soluble marker to mark tiny dots along the outside edge of each outer curve to denote placement of the leaves. Mark a tiny dot at the center position of each outer curve as well. Repeat for the four marked borders.

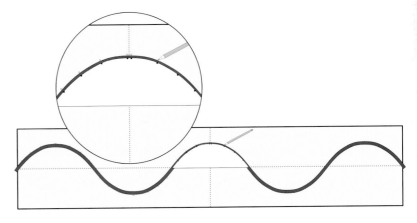

8. Use the stem placement guide to mark the position of the stems by placing it on each inner curve, with the point positioned

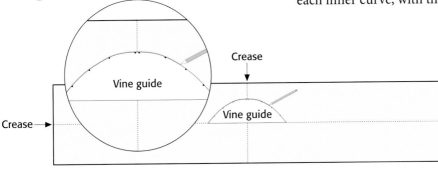

Crease

Vine guide

Crease →

Vine guide

at the marked center and the dashed line aligned with the center horizontal border crease. Mark each of the borders.

Stem placement guide

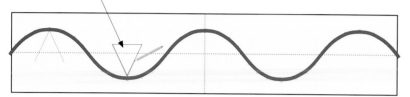

9. Place small dots of liquid basting glue along each marked stem line. Press a prepared 4½" stem onto each line, tucking the raw ends under the vine. Repeat for all four borders.

10. Referring to "Invisible Machine Appliqué" on page 28, stitch the vines and stems positioned on each border strip.

11. Lay out 10 prepared A appliqués on a border strip, and pin or baste in place. Stitch the appliqués and remove the paper pattern pieces. Lay out and stitch 10 B appliqués in the same manner.

12. Lay out 48 prepared C appliqués and 30 prepared D appliqués along the vines and stems. Use the marked dots for placement of the leaves.

NOTE: Take care not to place any leaves in the seam allowances where the border strips will be joined to the quilt center.

13. Referring to "String Appliqué" on page 30, stitch the appliqués in place. Lightly blot the water-soluble dots with a damp piece of white paper towel or muslin to remove them.

14. Repeat steps 11 through 13 to appliqué all four border strips.

Appliquéing the Border Corner Blocks

1. Press a diagonal crease in each cream print 10½" square.

2. Position a wreath placement guide onto a square, centering it over the pressed diagonal crease and placing the lower edge approximately 4" up from the bottom corner. Use a water-soluble marker to trace around the template, leaving the top area open as indicated.

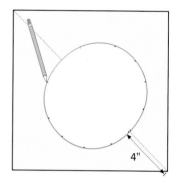

3. Place small dots of liquid basting glue along the marked line, leaving a small area at the bottom crest of the curve free of glue. Beginning at one end of the marked line, press a prepared 18" vine length down onto the glue, easing the vine around the curve.

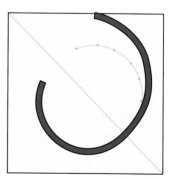

4. Place small dots of basting glue on the wrong side of a 3½" prepared stem and press it onto the creased center line of the block, tucking the raw end under the vine. Stitch the vine and stem in place.

5. Lay the wreath placement guide over the stitched vine and stem and use a water-soluble marker to mark tiny dots on the outside of the vine to denote placement of the leaves.

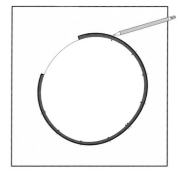

6. Working from the bottom layer to the top, lay out and stitch three each of prepared A and B appliqués.

7. Lay out 12 prepared C appliqués and 8 prepared D appliqués along the vine and stem, using the marked dots for placement of the leaves and overlapping them as necessary onto the vine to fit them well. Pin or baste, and then stitch in place.

8. Remove the water-soluble dots by lightly blotting them with a damp piece of white paper towel or muslin.

9. Repeat steps 2 through 8 to make four appliquéd corner blocks.

Assembling the Quilt Top

1. Referring to the diagram below, sew an appliquéd border strip to the right and left sides of the quilt center. Carefully press the seam allowances toward the border strips, taking care not to apply heat to the appliqués.

2. Sew an appliquéd corner block to opposite ends of the remaining border strips. Press the seam allowances toward the border strips, again taking care with the appliqués.

3. Sew a pieced border strip to the top and bottom of the quilt. Carefully press the seam allowances toward the border strips. The quilt top should measure 70½" square.

COMPLETING THE QUILT

Refer to "Finishing Techniques" on page 18 for details as needed. Layer the quilt top, batting, and backing. Quilt the layers together. The featured quilt was machine quilted in an heirloom style, with a teardrop medallion stitched in the open block areas and in several places along the border. A crosshatch pattern was stitched in the center of each patchwork block, and the remaining open areas of the quilt were filled in with very tiny and close stipple quilting. Join the 2½" strips of assorted dark prints into one length and use it to bind the quilt.

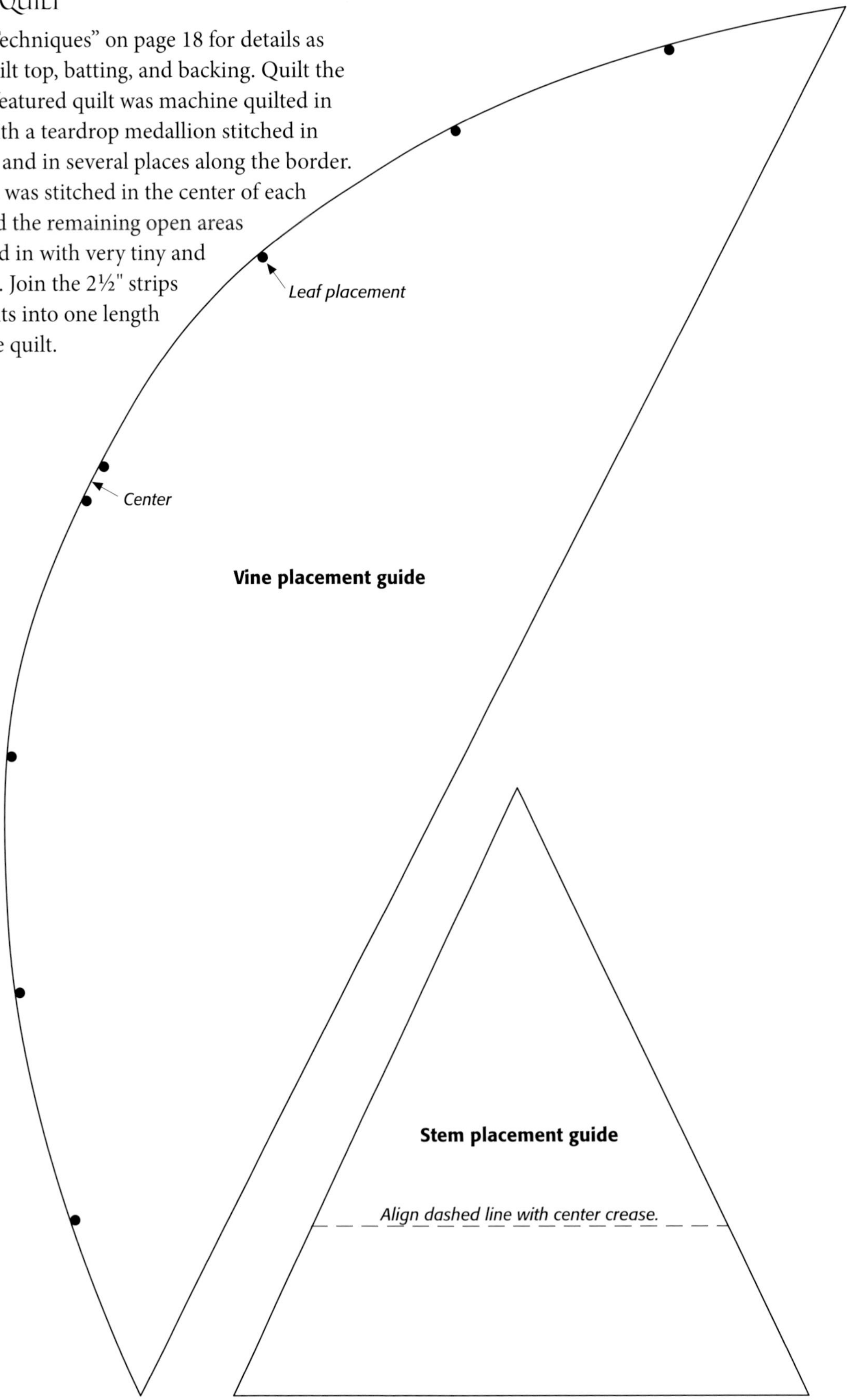

Leaf placement

Center

Vine placement guide

Stem placement guide

Align dashed line with center crease.

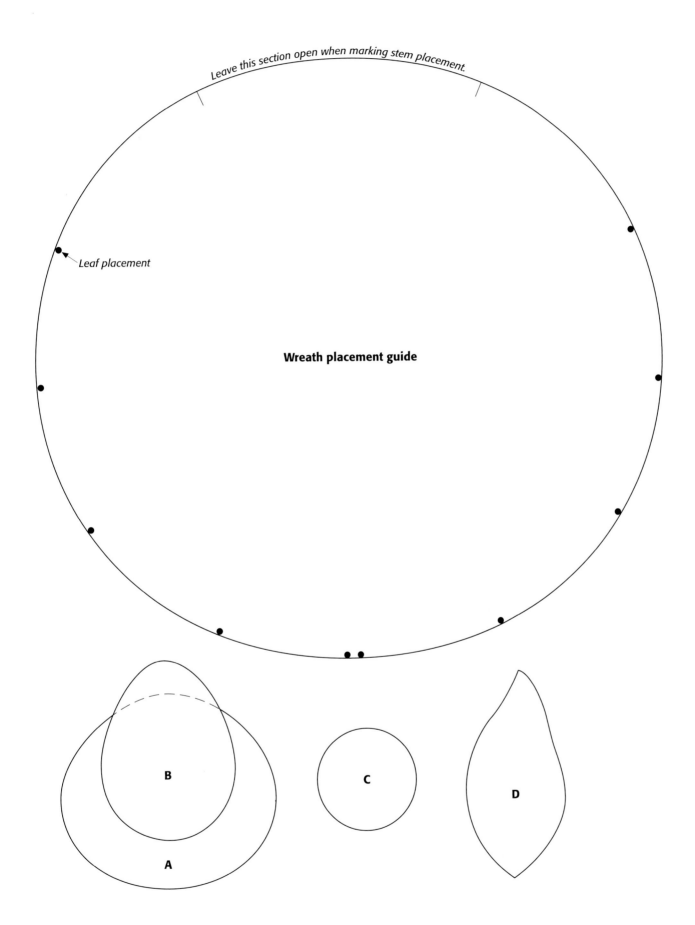

Leave this section open when marking stem placement.

Leaf placement

Wreath placement guide

A

B

C

D

ABOUT THE AUTHOR

As a young girl, Kim Diehl slept under her grandmother's hand-pieced quilts, but it wasn't until 1998 that she discovered quiltmaking for herself. From her very first quilt, Kim felt the urge to redesign elements of the project so that it would be a reflection of her own tastes and personal style. She finds that with the creation of each new quilt, her love of the design process continues to grow and flourish.

After winning *American Patchwork and Quilting* magazine's "Pieces of the Past" quilt challenge in 1998, Kim began designing quilts professionally and has seen her work published in several national magazines. She continues to design projects for the readers of *American Patchwork and Quilting*, and she has traveled to various parts of the country teaching her quiltmaking methods. *Simple Traditions* is Kim's second book with Martingale & Company.

Kim and her family make their home in Idaho, where they enjoy the clear blue skies and simple lifestyle that living in the Northwest brings.